THE KNIGHTS TEMPLAR

THE KNIGHTS TEMPLAR

FROM CATHOLIC CRUSADERS TO CONSPIRING CRIMINALS

MICHAEL KERRIGAN

amber
BOOKS

First published in 2019

Published by
Amber Books Ltd
United House
North Road
London N7 9DP
United Kingdom
www.amberbooks.co.uk
Instagram: amberbooksltd
Facebook: www.facebook.com/amberbooks
Twitter: @amberbooks

ISBN: 978-1-78274-757-4

Project Editor: Michael Spilling
Designer: Hart McLeod Ltd
Picture Researcher: Terry Forshaw

Printed in China

Contents

Introduction 6

1. The First Knights 26

2. Sworn to Serve 60

3. Holy War, Unholy Shambles 80

4. Might and Mystique 110

5. Before a Fall 134

6. Siege Mentality 166

7. A Long Retreat 190

8. The Stuff of Legend 210

Bibliography 218

Index 219

Picture Credits 224

INTRODUCTION

Strange as it might seem, the idea of religious monks fighting as warriors made sense to a medieval Christendom that felt that its frontiers – and faith – were under siege.

L ITERALLY A boy sent to do a man's job, Baldwin IV (1161–85) hadn't fared too badly in the circumstances. He'd been crowned King of Jerusalem in 1174, aged just thirteen. Starting as he meant to go on, he'd immediately mounted a large-scale attack on Damascus, availing himself of acrimonious divisions among the region's Muslim leaders. Baldwin's raid had been a triumphant success: he'd returned, his troops laden down with treasures – and the glory of having smashed the Saracens in their capital.

Ironically, the defeat he'd inflicted, compounding existing confusions and deepening rifts, had helped to sweep the charismatic Kurdish leader Salah ud-Din (1137–93) to power as sultan. In years of campaigning, 'Saladin' had already shown himself an inspirational leader and a general of flair and daring.

Opposite: As the scriptural scenes in this representation of Jerusalem's Crusader capture (1099) make clear, the medievals saw nothing oxymoronic in the term 'Holy War'.

Above: The seals of
Latin Jerusalem's King
Baldwin IV.

Now he was the master of the Muslim Middle East. On the face of it, he was much more than a match for the most precocious teenage hero. Baldwin's task was only going to get more challenging.

In any case, the Frankish ruler had other difficulties to contend with. He has gone down in history as the 'Leper King'. Although his condition had been clear since his early teens, its more unsightly symptoms had been slow in showing. Gradually, though, they were beginning to take hold. By his sixteenth birthday, while his face was still for the most part clear, his other extremities were swollen and scabbed with weeping lesions. He was still a warrior-king, however; still resolute in leading his forces from the front – even if his feet and hands had to be bandaged up beneath his battle armour.

JERUSALEM IN JEOPARDY

Baldwin didn't have much choice, in fact: the Crusader Kingdom of Jerusalem, established in 1099 after the successful First Crusade, was directly threatened by the rise of Saladin. For any Islamic ruler in the region, the very existence of a realm like this was an irritant; Christian proprietorship over Jerusalem not just an anomaly but an affront. It had been from the top of the Temple Mount that the Prophet Muhammad had made his *Mi'raj* – his Night Journey to Heaven. The Al-Aqsa Mosque still marks the site of his ascent. Saladin's hold over Egypt and Syria now firmly established, the re-taking of Jerusalem was his obvious next step. Piety, patriotism and the will to power all demanded it.

So it was that November 1177 saw Saladin once more on the move, with an army some 26,000 strong, heading for the fortified city of Ascalon (now Ashkelon, on the coast some 50km (30 miles) south of Tel Aviv). Baldwin, seeing his intentions, took several hundred knights to see to Ascalon's preservation. Saladin simply switched his objective: realizing that Baldwin's dash to defend the coastal city had left Jerusalem itself unguarded, he turned in his tracks to advance upon the Holy City.

Baldwin was unfazed. Calling together his 370 European knights, he also marshalled anything up to 4000 infantrymen, and 'turcopoles', raised from among the Christianized Arab population locally. Lightly-armoured cavalrymen, they matched the fighting style of the Saracens themselves, wielding scimitars or shooting arrows on the move. All in all, a significant force, then – though it was far outnumbered by Saladin's, by now advancing on Jerusalem at a complacent stroll.

Baldwin knew he was outnumbered – by rational standards, impossibly so. But that doesn't appear to have bothered him unduly. Ralph de Diceto (Ralph of Diss), who provided the most authoritative account that history has of these events, was a cleric himself, so wrote with a certain bias, it might be argued. Even so, his account of Baldwin's leadership, and the implicit trust he placed in God's support, still chimes with what we know of the young king.

Relying not on spears and swords, bows and arrows, but only on the aid of divine piety, armed and inspired similarly by the sign of the Lord's cross, his men made haste by night to meet the Saracen; remembering that it is easy for a multitude to be pinned down by a few, and that in the eyes of God there is no difference between winning among many or among few.

Below: Built around the height from which the Prophet Muhammad made his 'Night Journey', the Al-Aqsa Mosque ranks among Islam's most sacred shrines.

The king and his crusaders caught up with the Saracens some miles inland at Montgisard, near modern-day Ramla. Saladin's army seemed vast, spread out as it was across the open plain. The Franks appeared to be outnumbered a hundredfold. On the other hand, it was evident that no attack was anticipated. Rather than rushing forward to press the advantage of surprise, however, Baldwin called his army to a halt.

FALSE CONFIDENCE, TRUE CROSS

A chaplain walked out before Baldwin's assembled force. All uncovered and bowed their heads while he held up the sacred reliquary in which a fragment of the 'True Cross' was reverently housed. Its ornate golden work blazed like the sun. The relic within, to all appearances, was nothing more than a wooden splinter. It was, however, believed to have come from the actual cross on which Jesus Christ, the Crusaders' Saviour, had been crucified. No one could look upon it and remain unmoved.

Below: Crusaders inspired by the True Cross, as imagined in the nineteenth century by Gustave Doré (the 'real' relic wasn't much more than splinter-sized).

The Leper King knelt down, made the sign of the cross and gazed up devoutly at the blessed relic, uttering a pious prayer under his breath. He offered his own life – should it be required – in Christendom's cause. He begged, however, that God would give him victory over the infidel, for the sake of his believers and his Church. With the Lord's assistance, Baldwin and his forces would maintain and strengthen their hold over those Holy Places in Palestine in which – according to his sacred scripture – Christ had walked. Only when this devotional duty had been done did he at last order the attack upon the Saracens – who had now had several precious minutes to prepare.

No modern reader will be surprised to learn that Baldwin's charge was readily rebuffed. The Saracens formed a solid front against their enemy's advance. Vast as it was, however, Saladin's force was still widely dispersed across a considerable area of country. It wasn't really battle-ready; its leaders were comfortably at their ease. They didn't expect to have to fight in earnest until they reached Jerusalem. They were quite unready for the attack that now took place.

TEMPLAR TIME

Ralph de Diceto describes what happened when at this point a unit of Knights Templar entered the fray. Though dressed and armed as mounted knights, they'd taken vows as monks, in token of which their steel cuirasses were covered by snow-white mantles, surmounted by the bright red cross of their religious order. There were 84 of them in Baldwin's army, led by their Grand Master, Eudes de Saint-Amand (1110–79). At his command, they formed their four ranks up into a single wedge-shape as they cantered forward. Then:

Spurring all together, as one man, they made a charge, turning neither to the left nor to the right. Recognising the battalion in which Saladin commanded many knights, they manfully approached it, immediately penetrated it, incessantly knocked down, scattered, struck and crushed.

The Saracens, Ralph de Diceto continued, were 'dispersed everywhere; everywhere turned

Below: Saladin fleeing the scene of his abject humiliation at Montgisard, by an unknown artist of the nineteenth century.

in flight; everywhere given to the mouth of the sword.' The impact of the Templars' attack was as disproportionate as it was dramatic. 'One chased 1000, and two put 10,000 to flight,' Ralph says.

Poise personified as a general rule, the Saracens' leader was reduced to abject panic: 'Saladin was smitten with admiration, seeing his men dispersed,' we're told. 'He took thought for himself and fled, throwing off his mailshirt for speed, mounted a racing camel and barely escaped with a few of his men.' For Saladin's friend and biographer, Baha ad-Din (1145–1234), it was 'a disastrous event, a terrible catastrophe'.

DIVINE INTERVENTION

With the benefit of so many centuries of hindsight, it's easy enough for us to see how Eudes de Saint-Amand's Knights Templar were in the right formation at just the right time. And how overconfidence – and the sloppy deployment it allowed – undermined the strength of what should have been a far superior Saracen force. Those involved don't seem to have seen things that way, though.

If Baha ad-Din's impersonal language of 'event' and 'catastrophe' appears calculated to shift at least some of the blame from Saladin himself, Christian accounts seem no more eager to credit Baldwin with 'his' victory. If they do bestow praise on the young Frankish king, it's for the blessed favour he enjoyed in the sight of God: Montgisard was a triumph of strictly spiritual shock and awe. In their account, Baldwin's pause to display and venerate the True Cross relic is not a blunder but the essential prelude to a pious victory.

In making sense of Baldwin's win, we make calculations of psychology and tactical theory unavailable to a medieval mind that at the same time took the idea of divine involvement and intervention in its stride. These days, even devout believers by and large would not expect God to take a direct and immediate interest in such affairs of state or to enlist so obviously in forcing this or that outcome in the field of war. In the Middle Ages, it seemed natural enough that the God of Christendom would be a

Opposite: This engraving, based on Gustave Doré's drawing, shows the Saracen army broken by the charge of Eudes de Saint-Amand's Knights Templar.

partisan for his forces on the ground, just as the Muslims sought and expected Allah's backing. Hence the 'catastrophic' character of his defeat for Saladin – so much worse than a personal or political humiliation; a mark of divine displeasure, it must have seemed to him and to his men.

Baldwin's biographer, his former tutor William of Tyre (c. 1130–86), was so concerned that God should have the glory of the victory, the modern scholar Michael Staunton notes, that he made a point of remarking on the absence of important Christian fighters from the field. Listing several major figures who hadn't managed to make the battle – from the Prince of Antioch to the Counts of Tripoli and Flanders – he insists that this too had been divinely ordained. If they had been there, says William, the Christians might all too easily have concluded that 'Our hand has triumphed; the Lord has not done all this.'

OF MYTHS AND MEN

This account, as Staunton says, makes Montgisard a re-run of Gideon's triumph over the Midianites, in the biblical Book of Judges (chapters 6–8). There the Jewish leader's 300 men prevail over an enemy many tens of thousands strong – a clear example of God's favour towards his 'Chosen People'. In comparing Eudes de Saint-Amand with Judas Maccabeus, leader of a famous Jewish rebellion against Persian domination in 167–60 BCE, William was developing the same sort of parallel – even if Maccabeus belonged to the (mytho-)historical rather than the scriptural tradition.

Below: A symbol of revolt against religious repression, Judas Maccabeus became an inspiration for Christian Crusaders so many centuries later.

If God was intervening so directly in the affairs of mortal men and women, then none of the normal rules could be expected to apply. It wasn't just that the usual odds and probabilities were thrown into confusion so that there was 'no difference between winning among many or among few'. All the conventional rules were under suspension: a boy-king could be a match – and more – for an experienced and accomplished general; a powerful army put to flight by a comparatively trivial attack.

Indeed, if what was at issue was the greatness of God – rather than the drabber details of what we would now understand as history – then the weaker the instrument, the greater the glory to the Lord. The 'human factor' was all but absent. In allegorizing the achievements of men like Baldwin and Saint-Amand, the chroniclers may have been building up their heroic stature – but

Opposite: William of Tyre's chronicles reflected his role as tutor to the boy-king Baldwin IV. He later developed a bias against the military orders.

Below: St George and the Dragon, as shown in a mosaic at Maloula, Syria.

HOLY GHOST?

SEVERAL ONLOOKERS, shocked to see the Saracen army so unceremoniously routed at Montgisard, swore they'd seen them driven headlong by the mounted figure of St George. The dragon-slaying knight-at-arms was reputed to be buried not far away at Lydda (now Lod): why wouldn't he have risen from the dead to lend his assistance in this sacred cause?

His military valour, and his connections with the Holy Land, made George the obvious patron saint for the Crusaders. He was typically represented in art as a medieval-style knight. Longer-standing legends had always represented him as a Roman soldier – though by background he was believed to have been Greek. A convert to Christianity, he had supposedly been martyred for his faith at Lydda in an early persecution by the Emperor Constantine. Constantine the Great (c. 272–33) had of course himself later been baptized and

made Christianity the official religion of the Roman Empire. St George's shrine at Lydda had been built during his reign. (This great basilica still stands – though since the middle of the thirteenth century it's been a mosque.)

they were also, paradoxically, robbing readers of any real sense of these characters as men.

That men and women in the twelfth century saw things very differently than we do goes without saying. The depth of those differences is easily underestimated, even so. What are we to make, for example, of the Knights Templar, whose charge behind Eudes de Saint-Amand appears to have turned the tide at Montgisard? How do we account for their existence, even – a religious order, upholding Christian teaching, yet at the same time a company of knights? Highly trained, tightly disciplined and ready at a moment's notice to fight to the death for the Saviour who had blessed the 'peacemakers'?

IN ACCORDANCE WITH THE SCRIPTURE

Christ had of course been quite explicit in instructing his disciples to reject violence. 'Do not resist an evil-doer', he'd told his followers (Matthew 5, 39). 'If someone strikes you

Below: As this colourful – but bewilderingly violent – thirteenth-century miniature makes clear, the Middle Ages were a time of widespread war.

on the right cheek, offer him the other too' (Matthew 5, 39).
A few lines later, he'd summed up his doctrine in the form of
a new commandment: *Love your enemies* (Matthew 5, 44).
He had, of course, as unambiguously asserted that 'I bring
not peace, but the sword' – even if most scriptural scholars
assumed he was here speaking figuratively, referring to doctrinal
contention rather than to military conflict.

It was all a matter of interpretation, of course. The 'truth' of
the Christian scriptures may never have been up for doubt, but
that didn't mean complete and uncontested agreement about
what specifically they meant. Even the most honest and pious
readers could see things differently. The more learned
they were, indeed; the more complex and sophisticated
their scholarly perspective, the more difficulties they
tended to discern. Centuries of exegesis, far from
clarifying things, had underlined the ambiguity of all
linguistic utterance, the provisionality of the most
apparently definitive assertion.

> EVEN THE MOST HONEST AND PIOUS READERS COULD SEE THINGS DIFFERENTLY.

As for the moral universe: that was still less stable and secure.
In a real world in which evil didn't just exist but thrive, some
degree of compromise seemed called for. Christ's injunction to
'love our enemies' might make sense as a rule for the individual's
conduct of personal interactions – demanding as it was. But
could it seriously be said to be adequate as an approach to social
organization or statecraft? Was a Christian kingdom really
supposed to give free rein to murderers or violent brigands, or
allow itself – or its neighbours or allies – to be invaded?

WORD AND DEED

'In the beginning was the Word ...' says St John's Gospel (1, 1).
Where, however does the Word end and action for a Christian
(or a Christian polity) begin? Christ himself had highlighted
the problem: 'By their fruits shall you know them,' he'd said of
the 'false prophets' he expected to tempt his followers. What
mattered ultimately wasn't what they said but what they did.
Those actions had to take place in the real world, which meant
some recognition on the Christians' part of how that real world

Above: Knights Templar prepare to attack Jerusalem, from an eleventh-century manuscript.

worked. But the argument for a practical, realistic faith could quite clearly be an excuse for over-comfortable compromise. With its rich and powerful papacy and its far-reaching network of alliances with temporal rulers, the Church of Christ could be criticized on just these grounds. Even at this time, some argued for a more wholesale and whole-hearted rejection of 'the world'.

That same continuing tension has exerted its pull throughout the whole of Christian history. For many, Christ's message has seemed at its heart to be anarchistic in its tendency – a turning away from the great structures of conventionally established state and society, with all the inequalities and injustices that attend on them. Seeing the pomp and opulence surrounding so many religious leaders, Christians have often found themselves drawn to the idea of a stripped-down, 'back-to-basics' faith that would be closer to the Gospel ideal.

The Church, as through the Middle Ages it grew in worldly wealth and political power, clearly compromised the integrity of the creed of Christ. There's no disputing that many of its leaders displayed immense hypocrisy and cynicism, enriching and empowering themselves at the expense of their believers – and, ultimately, with the Reformation, of their faith.

A WAR FOR PEACE

If religion was to make a difference in the world, it had to engage with worldly issues and institutions. Those movements – pure in spirit as they may have been – that sought to opt out of society and its everyday affairs were by their very nature exceptional. Their viability arguably depended on the existence of a more conventional and socially-conformist Christianity to kick against. Where they didn't dwindle quickly away, disappearing into utter irrelevance, it was by making some sort of accommodation with the ecclesiastical status quo. Hence the enduring influence of St Francis of Assisi (1182–1226). His mendicant 'Franciscan' friars

CHRISTIAN SOLDIERS

CHRISTIANITY's coming-of-age, the emergence of what had been a strange little Jewish sect as a great religion, had famously come under the Emperor Constantine the Great. Roman power may have been well past its height by the time he ascended the throne, but he still reigned over the world's greatest state – which was still the centre of a vast and mighty empire.

The Roman mindset had remained a military one, then, and it had indeed been the promise of victory in battle that had inspired Constantine's conversion. The night before the Battle of Milvian Bridge (312), it was said, he'd seen a vision of a great gold cross spanning the heavens above him, with the glowing legend *in hoc signo vinces* – 'in this sign you will prevail'. Loving one's neighbour was all very well, but ancient rulers were naturally disposed to judge their deities by their 'talismanic' strength – their ability to bring good fortune, or victory in war.

Constantine's adoption of Christianity as the official state religion of the Roman Empire may have 'made' it as a creed, but it also locked it in to a particular relationship with temporal power. That relationship was to remain in force throughout the Middle Ages – and arguably, in some societies, down to the present day.

Below: A sixteenth-century representation of the Battle of Milvian Bridge.

Right: St Augustine articulated a famous theory of the 'Just War'.

rejected all the status and comfort available to the wider clergy of the time, but never challenged the authority of the Church.

Nowhere did the tensions between the idealist and the realist strands in Christianity show more starkly than in the question of war, its rights and wrongs. How could it ever be justified?, asked the idealists. How could it not be?, the realists retorted. 'Thou shalt not kill,' the Old Testament commanded (Exodus, 20, 13); return good for evil, Christ had urged – but, many Christians now reflected, to let wickedness thrive was a wicked act itself.

The first and most influential attempt to formulate a coherent *jus ad bellum* (law of warfare) was made in the fifth century by St Augustine (354–430), the Bishop of Hippo, a coastal city in North Africa. Most famous for his *Confessions* (380), and for the contribution of a dark, unsparingly self-critical strand to

Christian consciousness, Augustine also explored a wide range of other issues.

Writing at a time when the Empire's capital, Rome, was under attack from a succession of barbarian invaders, he argued (in *De Civitate Dei*, c.420) that the spiritual City of God was similarly beleaguered. Like the individual conscience, besieged by a host of selfish, sinful desires, the Christian faith was being constantly assaulted too. Although Augustine saw the danger as coming as much from the Church's own internal enemies – heretics and reckless reformers – he saw foreign paganism as a threat as well. And while his deep spirituality and theological sophistication can't seriously be disputed, neither can the stark simplicity of his conclusion: Christian orthodoxy had to be defended fiercely, if necessary by force.

War as an end in itself was evil, but as the promotion of a better outcome it was not just defensible but vital. 'We do not seek peace in order to be at war,' he said, 'but we go to war that we may have peace.' The 'Just War', he argued, was one 'that avenges wrongs, when a nation or state has to be punished, for refusing to make amends for the wrongs inflicted by its subjects, or to restore what it has seized unjustly.'

As such it was the earthly instrument of a general, divinely

Below: An angel leads the Crusaders towards Jerusalem, in a Gustave Doré-inspired engraving.

originating morality – one which owed nothing to personal resentments or prestige. 'True religion', wrote Augustine, 'looks upon as peaceful those wars that are waged not for motives of aggrandisement, or cruelty, but with the object of securing peace, of punishing evil-doers, and of uplifting the good.'

The motive to war should, for Augustine then, be as far as possible impersonal. Those who fought should do so for principle rather than for pique or pride. An exacting standard morally maybe – but, as the modern theological scholar John Langan suggests, once met, one that absolved the individual fighter of real responsibility. There's little sense of Augustine's finding any dissonance in the idea of the Christian soldier killing in Christ's name. Basically, the Christian duty to 'turn the other cheek'

FOUNDED IN FAITH

OUTSIDE ORPHIR, on Orkney's windswept mainland, stand the ruins of a once-magnificent church, originally constructed in the early years of the twelfth century. Round in plan, it is known to have been inspired by the Church of the Holy Sepulchre in Jerusalem – itself believed to have been built over the last earthly resting place of Jesus Christ.

In 1111, Earl Haakon Paulsson had quarrelled with his neighbour Earl Magnus. The pagan Viking was, it's reported, angered as much by Magnus' Christian piety as by his refusal to give up his lands. In his fury, Haakon had given the order to his men to murder Magnus, who was accordingly to be revered as a martyr for his faith.

Haakon himself was so remorseful when he saw what he had done that he converted to Christianity himself and embarked on a pilgrimage to expiate his guilt. His journey took him from one end of the medieval world to the other, from Christendom's northernmost frontier to the Holy Land. He had this church built in commemoration on his return.

In a way we can only vaguely apprehend, the medieval spiritual order seems to have been constructed spatially. We see this in everything from the idea of pilgrimage (a geographical journey that in some sense enacts a personal, moral and spiritual one) to the ordering of Hell, Purgatory and Heaven in Dante's *Divine Comedy* (1320). Within this religious geography, Jerusalem clearly had a special place: its defence was seen as one of Christianity's central tasks. Haakon's pilgrimage to foreign climes had in its way been a sort of homecoming, his Orphir church a sacred souvenir.

is trumped by the higher cause of being instrumental in the enactment of the will of God. The let-off is especially striking given Augustine's notorious severity over personal morality, his belief that the individual soul is mired in sinfulness unless saved by God.

It's easy enough to see how, confronted with such arguments, the medieval believer might come to see such military service as redemptive in itself. How a young man in the Middle Ages might even feel positively impelled to enlist in what historians have described as 'penitential warfare'. There's no doubt that medieval knights did see service in the Holy Land as a kind of quasi-pilgrimage, their departure on crusade a spiritual quest.

PILGRIM SOULS

Modern scholars have rightly been concerned to strip away some of the myth-making that surrounded the Crusades in their own time and the idealizing views of a predominantly Eurocentric historiography in the centuries since. But if some degree of cynicism about these ventures is appropriate, the cruder debunkings of our day go much too far. Claims that they represented an 'imperialist' project on a par with nineteenth-century European colonialism rest on hopelessly caricatured views of both episodes.

Below: A priest rallies the ranks of the Crusaders.

The suggestion that, in any meaningful way, they anticipated the twenty-first century's alleged 'wars for oil' in the Middle East appear even more ludicrously far-fetched.

In any case, whatever underlying economic or political purposes we may imagine really motivated the West, we have no reason to doubt the authenticity with which the Crusaders thought they acted. Christian believers really did believe – not necessarily literally, to the letter of the Gospel Word, but in what they saw as its spirit they believed intensely. They appear to have believed implicitly that, their own eternal salvation being at stake, any sacrifice in the earthly life was well worth making.

Although it would be perverse to imagine that medieval men and women were any 'better' than us, or less prone than we are to self-serving cynicism or hypocrisy, we'd surely be wrong to doubt the deep conviction of their faith. That they didn't succeed in living up to their Christian ideals in all the details of their daily lives doesn't make their grander gestures of piety or penitence insincere.

THEIR OWN ETERNAL SALVATION BEING AT STAKE, ANY SACRIFICE IN THE EARTHLY LIFE WAS WELL WORTH MAKING.

CONFLICTS AND CONTRADICTIONS

Hence the readiness of so many young men to enlist in military orders like the Knights Templar – and their society's willingness to recognize this as a meaningful vocation. If from our perspective their lifestyle may seem self-evidently un-Christian, that view would quite clearly have disturbed and baffled them.

All the indications are, for that matter, that it would have been equally surprising to their Muslim enemies, for whom the duty of *Jihad* ('struggle') was freely assumed to include military resistance against un-belief. Modern Islamic scholars are at pains to point out that the word encompasses more intellectual and spiritual strivings too, and that it isn't a straightforward endorsement of the idea of 'holy war'. There's no doubt though, that since the Prophet's proclamation of his Islamic faith in the years following his first revelation of 610, his message had been carried far and wide through a succession of Arab conquests. By the end of the millennium, the Islamic world had extended from east to west through Central Asia, the Middle East, North

Africa and all the way up the Iberian Peninsula to the Pyrenees – and at times beyond.

The Christian West was bound to define itself, politically and culturally, against this 'Other' – just as the Islamic world feared and scorned the Christian *kafir* ('infidel'). Even when the two rival camps weren't openly and violently in conflict, a state of something like 'Cold War' was to prevail between them into early-modern times. The success of Geoffrey de Bouillon's First Crusade (1096–9) in reconquering Jerusalem had only intensified the enmity between Islam and Christendom.

If the Knights Templar's purpose seems contradictory, then, that's in large part because they embodied the contradictions of their time, one in which there was real fighting to be done in the name of a real faith. That the worldview they represented was profoundly problematic and ultimately unsustainable doesn't mean they didn't have a role in their historic moment – even if it helps explain the troubles they would encounter in the longer term.

Left: Christ was the implicit inspiration for every crusade. Here we see him literally leading, with sword and scripture.

1

THE FIRST KNIGHTS

Intriguing parallels between the chivalric and the clerical vocations made their combination almost inevitable in time.

A KNIGHT ther was, and that a worthy man …', wrote the English poet Geoffrey Chaucer in *The Canterbury Tales*, c. 1390: 'That fro the tyme that he first bigan/To riden out, he loved chivalrie,/Trouthe and honour, fredom [the word here means 'nobility'] and curtesye.' Knighthood is for us the stuff of literature and legend, but it was the stuff of history as well – even if the real thing didn't measure up to the romance in all respects. Chaucer's 'verray parfit, gentil knight' did assuredly exist – though there was much more to him than immediately met the poet's eye.

It's easier for us to appreciate this other, darker side of his than it was for medieval witnesses, perhaps. The purported magnanimity and generosity of the chivalric elite is shown up ironically by what we all too clearly see as the systematic

Opposite: Spiritual and secular authority come together in the person of Baldwin I – seen here entering Edessa, 1098.

Above: Formidably strong in the field of war but kind and courteous in his manner, Chaucer's Knight embodied the ideals of chivalry.

exploitation and oppression of the masses. Enormous economic inequality – and a system pretty much devoid of democratic freedom for the populace at large – would have had to underwrite the sort of social relations that helped to produce Chaucer's paragon. But we'd be wrong to write off his admirable qualities as merely made-up or mythic: there genuinely was a chivalric tradition in which valour and skill in war went along with courtesy.

KNIGHTLY VIRTUES

Days drilling in sword- and shield-play; practice in the saddle with lance and mace; their skills regularly tested in tournaments, if not actually in battle … Knights were professional soldiers, highly trained. But they were also supposed to be superbly well versed in a range of softer, more sociable accomplishments. The word 'gentle' itself was cognate with 'genteel' and 'gentility'; just as 'courtesy' came directly from the 'court' – that little social circle clustering around a king or leading lord. By the same token, 'chivalry' (from the French word *chevalier*, meaning 'horseman', or knight) towards women was also seen as a mark of superior breeding – both in upbringing and in ancestry. Again, the assumption was that the knight's courage and accomplishment in arms were what enabled him to exercise mercy, compassion and politeness, his mild-manneredness a measure of his strength.

The knight was supposed to be the protector of all the weak, but of women especially. Naturally enough, this had important implications for relations between the sexes. Chivalric society wasn't just about long evenings feasting and carousing with comrades, but gentler afternoons offering chaste compliments to fine ladies. 'Courtly love', as it has come to be called, had its own exacting etiquette. Highly stylized, it seems in the sources to have been as much about pursuit through poetic praise as about consummation, Sir Lancelot's adultery with Arthur's Queen Guinevere the exception rather than the rule.

An 'ideal', we say: it's no coincidence that King Arthur and his knights are 'legendary' or that their lives are chronicled in romance, not history. As time went on and the late-medieval world gave way to the early-modern, the chivalric tradition would struggle to sustain itself – even as an aspiration. Don Quixote de la Mancha, in the celebrated Spanish novel by Miguel de Cervantes (1547–1616), represents its inadequacy and its ultimate irrelevance. Through the High Middle Ages, however, from the tenth century through to the fifteenth, chivalry can be said to have been at least a 'real ideal'.

> THE CHIVALRIC TRADITION WOULD STRUGGLE TO SUSTAIN ITSELF – EVEN AS AN ASPIRATION.

Left: Chivalry was as much about social rank and sexual politics as warfare, as this scene from the fourteenth-century court of Burgundy reminds us.

For us, so many centuries later, the idea of the chivalric knight belongs firmly in the realm of romance: in the stories of the Arthurian cycle, most famously. Arthur's court at Camelot became the central setting for a large and colourful genre of romance literature in which the Knights of the Round Table had a starring role (shaped thus so as not to give any one knight any special precedence over his brothers).

Geoffrey of Monmouth (c. 1095–1155) described life at Camelot most memorably in his *Historia Regum Britanniae* ('History of the Kings of Britain', c. 1135), introducing a cast of characters who've remained familiar to this day, including Arthur himself, Queen Guinevere and Merlin the Magician. Geoffrey's version originates the idea that Arthur was the son of King Uther Pendragon, whose stronghold was at Tintagel, on northern Cornwall's rocky coast, and that he was to be laid to rest after his death on the mythic western isle of Avalon. But there were a great many other storytellers and stories too, relating the adventures of individual knights as they sallied forth from Camelot to do battle with wicked enchanters, monsters and giants.

Above: He himself led a quiet cleric's life, but Geoffrey of Monmouth's mythohistory has helped shape the way we see the Middle Ages.

The most common narrative form, the 'quest', in which an individual knight set out to fulfil some challenge, doubled as an allegorical journey of self-improvement and discovery. Quests were by their very nature also 'tests' of character, determination and loyalty. They were often undertaken either to expiate some personal guilt or to right some spiritual wrong or social injustice (rather as pilgrimages – and enlistment in the Crusades – were to do in real life). Sir Perceval's quest for the 'Holy Grail' (the chalice or salver

said to have been used by Christ and his Apostles at their Last
Supper in the Gospels) was memorably described by the French
writer Chrétien de Troyes at the end of the twelfth century, and,
in his poem *Parzival*, the German Wolfram von Eschenbach
(c. 1180–1220) some years later. Sir Gawain's journey to meet
the challenge of the Green Knight became the subject of a famous
Middle English verse romance (late-fourteenth century).

COURTLY LOVE … AND LOSS

In between their great adventures, the knights paid elaborate
court to ladies – invariably beautiful but by no means necessarily
kind or sympathetic to their admirers. The trope of the love-
stricken knight pining with unrequited love for his cruel
mistress became a cliché. Paradoxically, given these narratives'
deep preoccupation with the theme of love, their heroes were
predominantly chaste despite themselves.

But courtly love wasn't always ethereal; nor were the passions
by any means always pure: this amorous paradise was never quite
trouble-free. Chrétien was quick off the mark in introducing a
dissonant note with his story of Lancelot's love for Guinevere,
an adulterous affair at the very heart of Arthur's court.

There were countless other betrayals, jealousies and rivalries
as well: the Arthurian world was very much a 'fallen' one.
These stories couldn't have continued to entertain so many

Below: Perceval arrives at
Grail Castle: the flaw in
his sword (just above the
king's hand) stands for the
moral failings that have
slowed his quest.

over so many centuries if they hadn't offered real 'grown-up' reading. In this respect, as romantic as they were, they partook very vividly of real life – just as real chivalric life partook of the idealism of the romances. It went without saying that the true-life knights of medieval Christendom often fell far short of the code of conduct they were sworn to follow – but their lives were still constructed around that code.

Opposite: Lancelot and Guinevere, a Victorian view. The queen's body-language suggests that hers is a femininity of 'forwardness', and so of sin.

CHARACTER AND CLASS

The institution of knighthood still of course exists in the United Kingdom. The title is bestowed by the monarch as a mark of special service. Its endowment in return for work on the parliamentary select committee for road transport or for services to the electrical-appliance industry reflects the old tradition that commoners could be 'knighted' for deeds of special valour in the country's cause. The reality is that, whilst such knighthoods do seem to have been conferred historically, they were anything but the norm. Knighthood was as much about social rank as derring-do.

THE WARLIKE SPIRIT WAS ASSUMED TO GO ALONG WITH NOBLE BIRTH IN THE MEDIEVAL MIND.

Not that martial courage didn't matter. It was very much a part of knighthood – it's just that the warrior spirit was assumed to go along with noble birth in the medieval mind. The word 'noble' itself is now associated as much with moral character as with the social status it once went inseparably along with; so, as we've seen, is 'gentle'. The English word 'coward', meanwhile, applied indiscriminately up and down the social scale, comes from 'cow herd' – to the medieval mind, the low-born had no disposition to (nor, in social function, any need for) courage.

AN ARISTOCRATIC EDUCATION

Typically, the medieval knight was marked out for his vocation from his earliest childhood. As soon as he reached the age of seven (Aristotle's 'age of reason', ratified by the usage of the time), he would be sent to the castle of his father's feudal lord to serve as a 'page', waiting at tables, running errands and performing other simple tasks. In return, he'd receive an

ONE FOOT IN THE WORLD

OF ALL KING ARTHUR's knights, Sir Galahad was said to be the purest, chaste in feeling, thought and word and deed. Yet he had himself been born of an illicit union. His mother, Elaine of Corbenic, had been the beautiful daughter of a king: she hadn't expected to be passed over by any knight she wanted. Lancelot, however, had been staunchly faithful to his true love – even if she was actually his lord's wife. Elaine had tricked her way into Lancelot's bed, wearing a ring of Guinevere's in the dark bedchamber. Galahad had been the result of this sole encounter.

Time and again we find the medieval romances acknowledging the temptations of the secular world and – while recognizing, often vividly evoking, their power – rejecting them. In this respect, Sir Galahad is exemplary: his life story traced the passage from darkness, deception and sin to that saintly chastity he was to represent in his chivalric conduct.

Something of the same was true of 'courtly love' at large in poems and stories of this kind. As extravagantly emotional (and at times explicitly erotic) as they could be, they were in general highly rarefied,

tending towards a 'platonic' ideal barely distinguishable from celibacy. Another reason, perhaps, for the vocations of monk and soldier to have seemed like a natural fit with each other in medieval times in a way that they really don't to us today.

Right: Sir Galahad picks his way through an allegorical forest of fleshly temptation in this 1862 painting by George Frederic Watts.

elementary training in martial skills – in riding and weapons-handling, and in other gentlemanly pursuits like hunting and falconry. He was also expected to develop 'softer' skills – in literacy at the very least, but also quite possibly in poetry and music. And, of course, along with these he'd gradually acquire the manners that (in the words of William of Wykeham (1320–1404)) 'maketh man' and equip him to become a courtly 'squire' once he turned fifteen.

Above: A pageboy trains: by the time he had served as a squire and entered knighthood he would be versed in every aspect of court life.

The squire was expected to have reached an all-but-adult level in the warlike arts. He was attached to a knight – to whom he swore allegiance – as his right-hand-man. His inseparable companion, he would tend to the knight's clothes and clean his weapons and carry his kit when he rode with him off to war. At the age of twenty-one, the squire was finally ready to be knighted. This was a solemn ceremony, with strong religious overtones. The evening before, for instance, the postulant knight would take a ritually-cleansing bath, then keep a night-long vigil praying for strength and honour in his vocation. Only then would he be ready to be 'dubbed', kneeling before his king or queen, who, standing before him, holding out a sword, leaned down and tapped him on each shoulder with its naked blade.

This 'accolade' – from the Latin *ad* ('to') and *collum* ('neck') – was originally, it's believed, a matey bantering blow – to begin with, the king typically administered it with his fist. The exact

Opposite bottom: Arthur's round table avoided precedence being given to any knight.

details of the ceremony differed over time and to some degree from court to court: in its essentials, though, it seems to have been the same. Arising as a knight, he was committed to uphold the honour of his monarch – and his new status.

THE BENEDICTINE RULE

Below: A queen dubs a new knight.

An ecclesiastical equivalent of the chivalric court might arguably be found in the monastic communities of medieval Europe.

CONTINENCE AND COURAGE

IN MEDIEVAL TIMES AS in our own, sexual potency was seen as central to manhood, but it wasn't seen to be expressed in quite the way it might be now. Sexuality as an ungovernable force was associated with women – weaker and less capable beings who were accordingly in thrall to their desires. Chaucer's Wife of Bath, in her sexual rapacity, caricatures this view of femininity; Francesca da Rimini (1255–85), guilty of an illicit affair with the brother of her husband, who finally murdered both lovers, provides a darker, more tragic version. Dante, who features Francesca in his *Inferno* (V, 73–142), clearly regards her with the deepest sympathy, yet still sees her transgression as a terrible – and quintessentially feminine – offence.

Masculinity meant self-control, and since this was also a mark of nobility of mind, sexual restraint was very much one of the knightly virtues. Common soldiers might rape captive women, but no knight would lose control of his baser impulses to this extent (so, at least, it was conventionally assumed).

So the chivalric hero wasn't seen as being in any way diminished by the cold resistance of his lady to his pleading. (She in her turn didn't come across as unsympathetically as we might think.) By the same token, the masculinity of the monk or priest wasn't seen as being compromised by his chastity. Again, an at least analogous relationship was clearly growing between perceptions of knightly continence and clerical celibacy.

Christians had come together in groups since Jesus called his apostles about him. (King Arthur's celebrated 'round table' was widely seen as recalling the board round which Christ's company had sat for their Last Supper – at which, of course, they had also used the 'Holy Grail'.)

Sharing and co-operation, inherent in the Christian faith, had only grown more important as time went on and they'd been forced to find, if not safety, then at least some degree of mutual support, in numbers. Gradually, though, more elaborately structured communities had

been formed, often removed from the distractions and the temptations of urban society. St Benedict of Nursia (c. 480–534) had founded several.

The first, at Monte Cassino, south of Rome, opened in around 530, was organized in line with what he had articulated as the 'Benedictine Rule'. A strict regime, appointing established times for acts of collective worship, private prayer and study; it also included daily shifts of manual work. Benedict saw such toil as a way of praising God and suppressing personal pride. His monks followed the motto *Ora et labora*, 'pray and work', but didn't distinguish as sharply as we might between the two.

A semi-hierarchical structure set an 'abbot' in overall authority in daily affairs, though he had to be elected by the community at large. For key decisions, moreover, he had to consult with his wider community. Nor was he exempted from the normal obligations of prayer, worship and work. The Rule left nothing to chance: its clauses (some 73 in all) covered everything from liturgical forms to food and clothing.

The monk had to be prepared to brave a gruelling daily round of worship – even before he lifted a finger in manual work. The idea was to

Below: St Benedict's was the vision behind the whole monastic movement – and, ultimately, behind the military orders too.

Ausculta, o fi
praecepta ma
gistri

KEEPING TIME

'Seven times a day I praise you,' says Psalm 119. The *horarium*, or timetable of hours, the Rule laid down was relentless. Divided into units of roughly three hours each, it started at midnight, with *Matins* – the night office; resumed with *Lauds* (or 'praise') at 3 a.m.; and continued three hours later with *Prime* (so called because six was considered the first hour of the monastic day). All then gathered in the community's council chamber (or 'chapter house') for *Chapter*, the abbot's daily briefing on what had to be achieved and on any items of important news.

Between these overnight services, monks had to snatch what brief bouts of sleep they could. Their daylight work routines were also regularly punctuated by hours of worship: the *Terce* (that is, the *tertius*, or 'third' hour) was held at approximately 9 a.m., to be followed at the sixth hour by the service of *Sext* or midday prayer. Then, at the ninth hour – or 3 p.m. – came *None*, named for the Latin for 'ninth', after which came *Vespers*, the evening service, at six, and then, at nine, *Compline* – so-called because it 'completed' the monastic day.

weave his existence into what amounted to a single, continuous avowal of religious love. 'Rejoice always, pray without ceasing,' St Paul had urged his followers in his First Letter to the Thessalonians (5,16). Thanks to the monasteries' well-motivated, educated and enterprising workforces, their farms and fisheries thrived. So did other ventures such as brewing beer or making wine and other drinks.

WORK ETHIC

The monasteries quickly became important economic centres – and to those who had, more money was to be given. Wealthy lay-people made cash contributions to their coffers, or bequeathed gifts – from land to preciously wrought chalices or vestments – in return for the prayers they hoped would help secure or speed their own salvation as they lay languishing, paying for their lifetime's sins in Purgatory.

Later reformers would rightly be cynical about the wealth and power Christian Europe's great monasteries eventually accrued, but that didn't mean that they were just exploitative. As we've seen, the Benedictine Rule offered a basic spiritual template into which all sorts of manual work might readily be slotted, and any amount of genuine good was done.

The care of the sick was one obvious example. Any sizeable monastery would have to have an infirmary for its own sick in any case: why not one which opened its doors to the wider public? Such houses sprang up the length and breadth of Europe as the High Middle Ages wore on.

Right: Monasteries involved themselves in economic activities of many kinds. Here we see a monk engaged in brewing (c. 1400).

Jesus himself had healed the sick – and, famously, urged on his followers the duty of a wider hospitality: 'For I was hungry and you gave me food,' he'd told his disciples (Matthew 25, 35); 'I was thirsty and you gave me drink, I was a stranger and you welcomed me.' Asked by his astonished hearers when they'd done these things for him, he'd assured them, 'Whatever you have done for the least of my brethren, you have done it for me.' Soon hospices were becoming a feature of medieval life.

Below: As seen by the German artist Andreas Brugger, St Bernard of Clairvaux ministers to the sick.

CURE AND CARE

The hospices were, of course, limited in the amount of 'medical' attention they could offer. Such science as existed at the time was rooted in the physiological thinking of classical Greece and Rome and reliant on the idea that illnesses were prompted by imbalances of different 'humours' in the body. Ancient treatments such as bleeding (though they were to remain in use into the middle of the nineteenth century) would have 'worked' only with their placebo effect, but such establishments could still provide a great deal of comfort for the sick.

The need for this kind of care was especially apparent in a place like Jerusalem, where Christian wayfarers found themselves weary, weak and far from home.

There may have been monastic hospices here from as early as the seventh century.

'ON EARTH AS IT IS IN HEAVEN'

The closeness the Middle Ages saw between the chivalric and the religious lives found no clearer embodiment than Pope Leo IX (1002–54; reigned 1049–54). Born Bruno of Egisheim-Dagsburg in Upper Alsace – now northeastern France, but then part of the German-centred Holy Roman Empire – his father was a count, and cousin of Emperor Conrad II (c. 990–1039; reigned 1034–39), the founder of the so-called Salian Dynasty. Brought up from boyhood to serve the Church, he never lost sight of the importance of earthly power – or of religion's wider social role. As Bishop of Toul, he kept in touch with Emperor Conrad, as well as his son and successor Henry III (1017–56; reigned 1046–56) doing diplomatic services for both.

In modern eyes, Bruno/Leo had a clear conflict of interest. It has to be admitted, though, that he served both sides well. His drive against corruption, first, as Bishop Bruno, in Alsatian foundations and, ultimately, in his papacy, throughout the Church, was a clear attempt to break the hold of local lords. The sin of 'simony', the sale of religious offices, was of course of advantage chiefly to those local magnates whom it suited to have their own hand-picked men in place in a particular parish or monastery.

At this time, the Church did not set any strict rules against priests being married – even if celibacy was still very much the norm. So matrimonial alliances could be another means of securing and maintaining power within the clergy. Bruno pressed persuasively for clerical celibacy. (That Bruno had himself been the beneficiary of family connections appears only to

Above: Pope Leo IX, was to found the first military order in the *Milites Sancti Petri* ('Knights of St Peter'), 1053.

have underscored for him the dangers to the wider Church and Empire.) Altogether, although his reforms undoubtedly furthered the interests of his own connections in the Salian Dynasty, they helped to shore up the authority of Rome as well.

OF KEYS AND CONSTANTINE

St Peter's successor as the head of Christ's Church, the Pope is held to have inherited those powers Jesus invested in his leading apostle. 'You are Peter', the Lord had famously said (Matthew 16, 18), predicting his eventual death and resurrection and final departure from his disciples' midst; 'and on this rock …' (he punned on the Greek word *Pétra*, 'stone') '… I will build my Church.' Christ continued, conferring on Peter open-ended (if ill-defined) authority to lead in his coming absence: 'I give you the keys of heaven. Whatever you bind on earth will be bound in heaven; whatever you loose on earth will be loosed in heaven.'

> THE CATHOLIC CHURCH WAS COMING TO BE A SECULAR POWER IN ITS OWN RIGHT.

For Catholics, these lines licensed the absolute spiritual authority of the Pope – passed down the generations through the so-called 'apostolic succession'. But no one ever interpreted these lines as granting the Pope any secular authority on earth. 'Render unto Caesar what is due to Caesar,' Christ had said when asked if his followers should pay their taxes to the Roman Empire (Mark 12, 17), 'and to God what is due to God'.

For Leo IX, Christ and Caesar were to be two sides of the same coin. They were two sides of his own personal and professional formation, after all. Especially because, under his rule, the Catholic Church was coming to be a secular power in its own right within the wider Holy Roman Empire. Leo was an energetic promoter of the so-called 'Donation of Constantine' – a document supposedly drawn up at the request of the great Christianizing emperor and signed by him before he died. It was known as a 'donation' because it bequeathed extensive territories in central Italy to the Church, whose leader was to exercise temporal authority over them. This 'donation' looked dubious even then (it seems to have been a forgery, dating from the fifth century) – but Leo insisted on its authenticity. While it was to be definitively discredited in the fifteenth century, the Church ruled 'Papal States' in Italy well into the nineteenth (and of course holds sway in the Vatican City to this day). Leo led a double life as both spiritual pontiff and earthly ruler.

NORMAN CONQUESTS

In this latter capacity, at any rate, Leo was soon to be up against it. Ironically, from adherents of his own faith. For several decades now, Norman adventurers – descendants of Norwegian Vikings who'd settled in France and converted to Christianity there – had been passing through Sicily as pilgrims en route to the Holy Land. Much of southern Italy at this time was under Byzantine rule – or at least it was supposed to be.

Some decades earlier in Sicily, however, the Byzantine authorities had recruited the Normans as mercenaries to see off the Arab pirates who had plagued their shores. And, in fairness, the adventurers had delivered on that commitment. So comfortable had they come to feel in their new sunny southern home, however, that they'd settled down there and, essentially, refused to leave. Not just that, but they had been followed by waves of their younger kinsmen,

Below: Norman power in Sicily would reach its height in the twelfth century. Here, William II (1153–89) holds up his cathedral at Monreale.

who'd set about carving out little enclaves of their own on the Italian mainland to the north.

In 1053, then, at the height of the Byzantine Patriarch's religious dispute with Pope Leo IX, the Byzantine state appealed to its friend and ally Leo IX the quasi-king. The Byzantines asked for his support against an enemy which, as they pointed out, represented a threat to his territories in central Italy in the longer term.

Above: Defeated at Civitate, Leo IX received the Norman victors' homage – but they still took him prisoner, and helped themselves to much of his territories.

PAPAL FALLIBILITY

As comfortable in military command as in spiritual authority, it seems, Leo set about raising forces to resist this threat. While a coalition of allies, from the Lombards of northern Italy to the Swabians of southern Germany, contributed troops, the Pope created his own new order of knights to lead this army into action as its vanguard. Their title, the *Milites Sancti Petri* ('Knights of Saint Peter'), left ambiguous (perhaps deliberately) the extent to which they belonged to the Church as a whole and to which they might be seen as a sort of papal 'private army'.

With the Knights of St Peter at their head, this allied army met the Normans at Civitate (now known as San Paolo di Civitate),

THE OTHER 'OTHER'

WE'RE quick – and, admittedly, for the most part correct – to see medieval history working itself out as an opposition of two power blocs, centred respectively in the Christian West and an Islamic East. There were complicating factors, though; most obviously, perhaps, the emergence through the early Middle Ages of an alternative, eastern Christian tradition – one we'd later come to characterize as 'Orthodox' (though of course from a western, Roman Catholic perspective, orthodox was exactly what it was not).

Cultural and linguistic differences had caused the two halves of the old Roman Empire to diverge centuries before: the West had been European and Latin; the East Asiatic and Greek. The former Greek trading settlement of Byzantium, renamed Constantinople by the first Christian emperor (and subsequently, by Turkish invaders, Istanbul), had become the centre of an alternative eastern empire that was increasingly overshadowing the first one, around Rome. After Rome's fifth-century fall, this second empire had continued in its own established path: this Byzantine Empire was to last another thousand years.

For some time now, with the West in apparently terminal crisis, but their own fortunes buoyant, Church patriarchs in the East had seen no particular reason to bow and scrape before the popes. They owed political allegiance to the Byzantine emperors, who had the right of appointing them; their loyalty to the pontiff tended to take second place. The authority of Rome was recognized formally, but deference was offered more and more grudgingly as time went on.

In 1054, Rome decided that enough was enough and a bull (or official papal letter) from Leo IX denouncing the Patriarch, Michael Kerullarios, was placed upon the altar of Hagia Sophia, Constantinople's great basilica. Kerullarios responded in kind: before anyone knew it, Pope and Patriarch had excommunicated one another – expelled them from their church community. What became known as the East–West Schism was under way. From that time on, the 'Orthodox' Church of the East would exist entirely separately from the Catholic Church. Only in recent decades has a dialogue begun between the two.

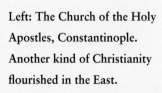

Left: The Church of the Holy Apostles, Constantinople. Another kind of Christianity flourished in the East.

north of Foggia. Devoted Catholics despite their waywardness, the Normans were genuinely reluctant to defy their pope, still less to attack him, but sneers from Leo's own troops appear to have goaded them into action.

It's not known how the Knights of St Peter acquitted themselves in this their first engagement – though the decisive defeat that their side suffered is perhaps a clue. Leo IX was actually captured, and although the Normans treated him with elaborate respect, he clearly experienced this as an enormous humiliation. And, deferential as they were to the Pope in person, they were much less scrupulous in respecting his territorial claims, extending Norman rule over much of southern Italy.

The Knights of St Peter disappeared from the historical record just about as abruptly as they'd entered it. But their founding idea was destined to endure.

GOD'S WILL

In the meantime, the whole of the western world was to be mobilized en masse, called earnestly to arms by Pope Urban II. The emergency was dire, he warned an electrified audience at the Council of Clermont, in November 1095. Islam's armies were massing on Christendom's very doorstep. Whatever our differences with the Byzantines, he urged, they were our brothers and sisters in Christ. Were we seriously going to stand by and see them enslaved, he asked – and by the infidel?

Fulcher of Chartres (1059–1128) recorded the occasion in his

Below: Urban II calls Christianity to arms at the Council of Clermont, 1095. His speech here was to inspire the First Crusade.

chronicle. Building his case for action in an oratorical crescendo, Urban brought his address to a climax with this urgent – even desperate – appeal:

For this reason I beg and urge you – no, not I, but God Himself begs and implores you, as the messengers of Christ, the poor and the wealthy, to rush and drive away this mob from your brothers' territories, and to bring swift assistance to those who also worship Christ.

He got the reaction he had been seeking: with one collective, clamorous voice, Fulcher reports, his assembled hearers bellowed 'Deus vult!' – 'God wills it!'

In the weeks and months that followed, in response to Urban's plea, Europe rose in an extraordinary ferment of Crusading zeal. Knights and soldiers were obviously galvanized, but ordinary men, women – and even children – of every sort were also swept up in the mania; all wanted to do their bit to defend their faith. They could only do this by winning back the Holy Places.

So, at least, the argument went. Jerusalem had actually been under 'infidel' occupation since its seizure in 638 in the first

Below: Jerusalem had been in Muslim hands since 638, when it had been taken by Caliph Umar (c. 584–c. 644; reigned 634–44).

Above: Peter the Hermit rallies the masses for his 'People's Crusade' (1096).

wave of Arab conquests. Since then, Christian pilgrims had for the most part passed back and forth unhindered. Now, with the Christian West under genuine geopolitical pressure across a wider front, though, access to the Holy City became a handy *cause célèbre*. These streets down which Jesus Christ had stepped; the Holy Sepulchre in which he had been (however briefly) buried … these surely 'belonged' to Christians by right?

A MOTLEY CREW

Among those who volunteered to go and fight, motives were inevitably mixed. Many must have been drawn by the prospect of plunder; many more, maybe, by the thought of an adventure, a break from a monotonous routine; but thousands were inspired by what they saw as a sacred duty. They were swayed as well by the Pope's promise of an indulgence for all who made the journey to Jerusalem: time off from the fearful sufferings of Purgatory.

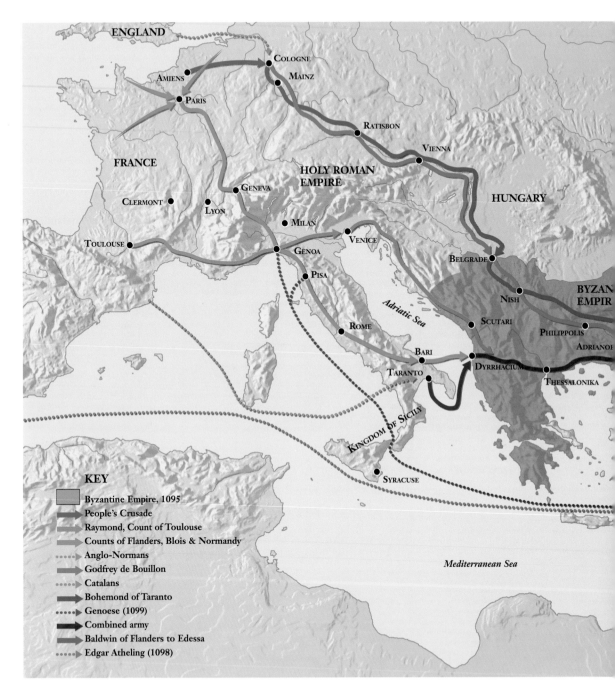

KEY

Byzantine Empire, 1095
People's Crusade
Raymond, Count of Toulouse
Counts of Flanders, Blois & Normandy
Anglo-Normans
Godfrey de Bouillon
Catalans
Bohemond of Taranto
Genoese (1099)
Combined army
Baldwin of Flanders to Edessa
Edgar Atheling (1098)

The fervour Urban had unleashed could not readily be contained. Peasants and poor workers were fired with religious zeal. A wandering preacher, Peter of Amiens, or 'Peter the Hermit' (c. 1050–1115), who started out in northern France, had soon raised a rag-tag 'army' up to 100,000 strong. Vague

THE FIRST CRUSADE – ROUTES OF THE CRUSADING ARMIES

Black Sea

SINOPE

TREBIZOND

'ANTINOPLE

CIVETOT

ANCYRA

SELJUK SULTANATE OF RUM

CAESAREA

LAEUM, 1097

PHILOMELIUM

MARA'

HERACLEA

EDESSA

ICONIUM

TARSUS

ANTIOCH

TRIPOLI

BEIRUT

SIDON

DAMASCUS

ACRE

JAFFA

ASCALON, 1099

JERUSALEM, 1099

DAMIETTA

ANDRIA

CAIRO

about exactly where they were going and who they believed they were about to fight, those embarked on this 'People's Crusade' pushed into western Germany, sacking synagogues and massacring Jews ('Christ's killers'). Only then did this rabble turn southeastward, raping and pillaging indiscriminately as they went: they were finally turned back by the Byzantine Emperor Alexius I.

A HARD SLOG

The 'official' Crusade, conducted by a largely French (so 'Frankish') army led by Godfrey de Bouillon (1060–1100), got off to a rather more promising start. The Crusaders quickly captured Nicaea, capital of the Seljuk Turks in what is now northwestern Turkey. As they fought their way over the

Left: This map shows the routes taken by the various Crusader forces to reach the Holy Land. Although France provided the bulk of the troops for the First Crusade, the Crusaders were a truly multinational force, with elements from England, Catalonia, Italy and the Rhineland.

Anatolian mountains into northern Syria, however, triumph turned slowly but inexorably into disaster.

Their expedition might have been months in the planning, but the logistical problems involved in getting a vast army – not just men (and women and children) but horses and beasts of burden

– across the arid terrain of central Turkey in a time of scorching heat soon proved all but insurmountable for the Crusaders. Many thousands expired in agony: of the 100,000 who had set out, only 40,000 arrived exhausted at the gates of Antioch.

That city, Syria's strategic centre, was formidably fortified: the Crusaders took it, but only after a seven-month-long and very costly siege. In June 1098, successful at last, they took out their anger on the captured city's inhabitants, many thousands of whom (including Christians) were massacred.

SANCTIFIED SLAUGHTER

Over the following year the Crusaders saw off a number of attacks from the Saracens, though they continued to take casualties all the while. By the time they were ready to advance on Jerusalem, in June 1099, their numbers had been reduced to 20,000. After another – this time much shorter – siege, Godfrey de Bouillon himself led the party which on 13 July found a

Below: The main routes taken by Christian forces in the First Crusade, and the leaders of the Third or 'Kings' Crusade.

Opposite: Baldwin II is crowned King of Jerusalem (1118), from an edition of William of Tyre's *Historia* published in the 1460s.

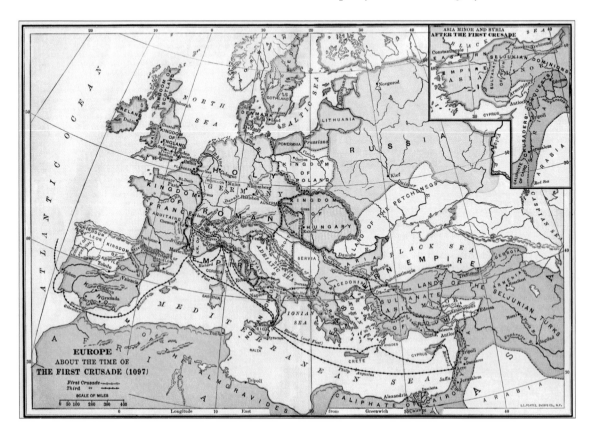

ANOTHER WORLD

THE CHRISTIAN PILGRIM COMING to the Holy Land might, in a spiritual sense, be 'coming home', but he or she was nevertheless stepping into another world. Islamic tradition – the *Koran* itself, indeed – demanded that the rights of other monotheistic believers (the 'Peoples of the Book') should be respected when they came in peace. And for the most part this convention had been upheld. Inevitably, though, there had been times of tension in which the visitors didn't feel quite so welcome. In addition, even at the best of times, there were other hazards to be negotiated, ranging from roadside bandits to linguistic difficulties.

That the less educated were liable to leave their homelands with very little conception of either the distance they had to travel or the alienness of the country they were headed for meant that many arrived in a weak and vulnerable state. It appears that, from as early as the seventh century, steps had been taken by religious groups to offer emergency shelter and rudimentary medical assistance in the most extreme cases.

way over the walls and breached Jerusalem's defences. They celebrated their triumph with a veritable orgy of killing in the city.

Raymond of Aguilers' claim that they rode through the city streets 'in blood up to their bridle reins' would seem self-evidently exaggerated, though the unanimity among Christian chroniclers about the commission of atrocities is still striking.

It's hard for us to know whether they were writing in disapproval or enthusiasm (at this historical distance, we can't judge the tone). Their shock at the scenes unfolding remains clear, though. 'No one had ever heard of such a bloodbath among pagan peoples as this one,' wrote William of Tyre. 'If you had been there,' wrote Fulcher of Chartres, 'you would have seen our feet stained to our ankles in the blood of the slain … None of them was left alive; neither women nor children were spared.'

The First Crusade had secured its objectives. The Holy
City became the centre of its own little state, the Kingdom of
Jerusalem, over which, from 1100, King Baldwin I (c. 1060–
1118) held sway. A palace was constructed for him round the
citadel, or 'Tower of David' – a fortress already dating back
(as its name suggests) over several centuries.

Three further 'Crusader states' were now established in the
wider Middle East: the Principality of Antioch, and the Counties
of Edessa and Tripoli (in northern Lebanon). These became
important centres for commerce and culture between East
and West.

From the modern perspective, it's tempting to see these
states as 'colonies' – and in a sense they were' except that the
overwhelming superiority in wealth, technology and military
strength the European powers were to enjoy over their subject
nations in the nineteenth century was absent here. If anything,
it was the other way round. By the standards of an Islamic
world, which was way ahead in science and learning, the
'Franks' really were the rude 'barbarians' the Muslims saw them
as. Be that as it may, they were in charge – at least for now.

FRONT-LINE FEUDALISM

The so-called 'feudal' system, in force across Christian Europe
through much of the Middle Ages, was in its origins essentially
military – colonialist, as we might call it – a way of bringing
wide areas of occupied territory under a ruler's sway. Although
in its details it differed from place to place and developed
complex refinements over time, it hinged on the exchange of
loyalty for land. A king made grants of territory to trusted
henchmen, who enjoyed great power as local lords – and
wealth, because they could keep much of the agricultural
production of their lands. As vassals – sworn supporters –
however, they owed the king fealty (or loyalty). They were
committed to provide their own armed assistance, and that of
their men, in his service should this be required.

In Europe, as time went on and, for lengthy periods, peace
prevailed, the warlike foundations of the system could for the

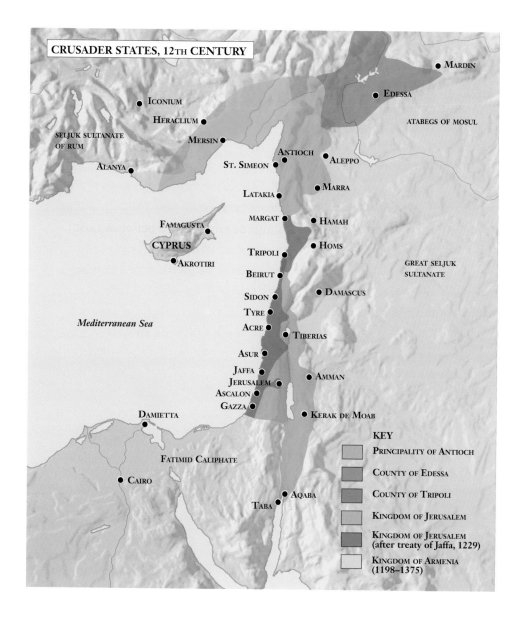

CRUSADER STATES, 12TH CENTURY

MARDIN

ICONIUM

EDESSA

HERACLIUM

ATABEGS OF MOSUL

SELJUK SULTANATE
OF RUM

MERSIN

ANTIOCH

ALEPPO

ALANYA

ST. SIMEON

MARRA

LATAKIA

MARGAT

HAMAH

FAMAGUSTA

CYPRUS

TRIPOLI

HOMS

AKROTIRI

BEIRUT

SIDON

DAMASCUS

Mediterranean Sea

TYRE

ACRE

TIBERIAS

ASUR

JAFFA

AMMAN

JERUSALEM

ASCALON

GAZZA

DAMIETTA

KERAK DE MOAB

KEY

FATIMID CALIPHATE

PRINCIPALITY OF ANTIOCH

COUNTY OF EDESSA

CAIRO

COUNTY OF TRIPOLI

KINGDOM OF JERUSALEM

AQABA

KINGDOM OF JERUSALEM
(after treaty of Jaffa, 1229)

TABA

KINGDOM OF ARMENIA
(1198–1375)

most part disappear from view. They never did entirely. Then as
always, competition between rival states invariably generated
friction. And, of course, the existence of a warrior elite at the
top of every major kingdom more or less guaranteed its flaring
up into all-out war. The rest of the time, though, it was possible
to see the role of the monarch as largely ceremonial; that of the
armed aristocracy as ornamental.

In a Holy Land so hard and recently won back from Islamic
occupation, there was no disguising the nature of the western

presence. Kings of Jerusalem ensured the presence of sufficient 'boots on the ground' by dividing their realm into smaller lordships or *seigneuries*.

The principality of Antioch and the counties of Edessa and Tripoli to the north technically lay outside the Kingdom of Jerusalem – though they owed fealty to its king. Within the Kingdom's territories were the Principality of Galilee (in turn divided into lordships of Beirut, Nazareth and Haifa), the Lordships of Sidon and Oultrejordain ('Transjordan', as it would much later be called – lands lying on the eastern banks of the famous river), along with a host of smaller seigneuries.

ST JOHN'S HOSPITAL

The Hospital of St John of Jerusalem (so called because it occupied the site of a former monastery dedicated to St John the

Below: By the nineteenth century, the site of St John's Hospital had become the Muristan (the Persian name means 'hospital'), a market quarter.

Baptist), just to the south of the Church of the Holy Sepulchre, seems to have opened its doors in the aftermath of the First Crusade. Or perhaps it just grew in size and formalized its status at this point. Generous gifts from influential donors are recorded at this time. (Like other monastic foundations, the Hospital was the beneficiary of wealthy men's anxiety that their earthly actions hadn't been quite good enough in themselves to ensure their speedy progression from Purgatory to Paradise.) Godfrey de Bouillon gave them his claim over the rents from Hessilia, a Palestinian village that had come to him as spoils of war. Other offerings came flowing in thereafter.

It's hard to be sure exactly how the Hospital's first few years of history unfolded. We know that the Pope recognized the Hospitallers' work – and their status as an independent order – in 1113. Beyond that, though, the narrative is vague. The early chroniclers' industry in cooking up a fanciful mytho-history (including claims of a much earlier – even a pre-Christian – foundation) hasn't made it any easier to trace the real story. The likelihood is that the Order was for several decades more monastic than military in its emphases.

THE LIKELIHOOD IS THAT THE ORDER WAS FOR SEVERAL DECADES MORE MONASTIC THAN MILITARY IN ITS EMPHASES.

That said, Jerusalem wasn't any ordinary city, and St John's monks would have certainly had to care for pilgrims and soldiers killed in skirmishes with Saracens in the surrounding country. Although the Holy Places were now in Christian hands, their hold was anything but secure; the stability of previous centuries was accordingly at an end. For now, at any rate, the monks of the Hospital don't seem actually to have involved themselves in any of the fighting; they were nevertheless kept occupied tending the wounded.

TO ARMS

It was rapidly becoming clear, however, that any meaningful care for the welfare of Christian pilgrims to the Holy Land would require some attempt to protect them while they were making their way through what was still a hostile countryside to and from Jerusalem. By now well-funded by their western backers, the monks of the Hospital were, by the beginning of the twelfth century, employing mercenaries to escort parties of pious travellers to and from the coast.

We don't have a reliable date for the arming of the monks themselves, as the 'Knights Hospitaller', though they seem to have been functioning as a military order by the 1130s. Neither do we know how or why the shift in focus took place – was this no more than medieval 'mission creep' or a conscious and deliberate change of direction on their part?

As we've seen, this new departure wouldn't have seemed as shocking to the medieval mind as it might to the modern. The Hospitallers were quite at home with St Augustine's 'Just War' theory. We've also seen, in the present chapter, a range of ways in which the religious and the chivalric order would have seemed analogous – just different ways of going about God's work.

WHERE THERE'S A WILL

The Hospitallers were beneficiaries of the euphoria following the 'freeing' of Jerusalem. The eyes of Europe were on the Middle East. Donations to religious orders were, as we've seen, an accepted part of medieval life. Now a great many men of wealth – whether actual or 'armchair' Crusaders – were keen to see their dying legacies directed towards the continuation of the Christian war-effort in the Holy Land.

Below: Raymond de Saint-Gilles (c. 1041–1105), Count Raymond I of Tripoli, built this citadel at the start of the twelfth century.

Their sons, on attaining knightly status, were eager to sign up with one of these heroic orders – and, when they did, they conventionally came accompanied by lavish gifts. As important as their personal military service might prove to the Hospitallers over time, their immediate contribution was financial. All the more reason for the Hospitallers to accentuate the military aspects of their mission: that was where the aristocratic recruits – and hence the rich endowments – were.

Above: Raymond de Saint-Gilles' citadel in Tripoli was one of a chain of Crusader castles in the Holy Land.

Once they'd embarked on the military course, there was no going back. Further gifts only underlined their new fighting role. When, in 1136, King Fulk of Jerusalem (c. 1090–1143; reigned 1131–43) offered them the castle of Beit Jibrin, not far from Hebron, for example, were the Hospitallers really going to say no?

Consequently, it only made sense to say yes when, six years later, Count Raymond II of Tripoli (c. 1116–52; reigned 1137–52) gave them a chain of further fortresses along his borders. Raymond's Tripoli (the name of course just means 'Three Cities') was in Lebanon, and not to be confused with the now-more-celebrated Libyan port, so these borders were in what we now think of as Syria.

Crac des Chevaliers, Castellum Bochee, Lacum, Felicium and Mardabech: these were all strategically important at the time. Raymond's bounty, by his own admission, was rooted as much in tactical sense as piety, then: he needed assistance in defending his territories against Islamic raiders. But since these castles came with the rights to land and trade in the towns of Baarin and Rafaniyah, the Knights Hospitaller saw it as a rich opportunity.

2

SWORN TO SERVE

The military orders may have been 'bound' to Christ, but their concerns were often earthly, their rivalries at times with each other, their loyalties to themselves.

THE HOSPITALLERS' militarization may have been accelerated by the growth in competition from the Knights Templar in the years following their foundation. At Easter 1119, a party of pilgrims headed out from Jerusalem to visit the banks of the River Jordan, where Christ had been baptized (Matthew 3, 13–17), was attacked by Saracens, and anything up to a hundred men and women massacred. Feelings at the Christian court were naturally running high, and many felt that some direct response was needed.

PROTECTING THE PILGRIMS

At the very least, protection had to be afforded to those who'd come so far in peace to do reverence in the homeland of the Lord. To some extent, of course, such a service was already being provided by the Knights Hospitaller, but their resources were still

Opposite: Enmity with Islam was by now well established in western tradition. Here, Charles Martel stops the Moors' advance into France at Poitiers in 732.

scant, and their coverage patchy, as the Jordan incident showed. So, in the words of William of Tyre:

> *… certain noble men of knightly rank, religious men, devoted to God and fearing him, bound themselves to Christ's service … They promised to live … without possessions, under vows of chastity and obedience. Their foremost leaders were the venerable men Hugues de Payens and Godfrey de St Omer. Since they had no church or fixed abode, the King gave them for a time a dwelling place in the south wing of the Palace, near the Lord's Temple.*

Hence their name, of course. The gift from King Baldwin II (?–1131; reigned 1118–31) was to be a lifeline to De Payens (c. 1060–1136), the Order's founder and first Grand Master. Till then, it's said, they had been so poor that De Payens and his friend and comrade De St Omer had been forced to share a single horse – a fact subsequently commemorated in the Knights Templar's seal.

The Order's purpose, William of Tyre continued, was that of protecting the roads and routes against attacks from robbers and brigands. This they did especially to safeguard pilgrims. This made them very much like the Knights Hospitallers, now that they no longer focused solely on the sick. While they served the same cause, the two orders were soon in competition.

Right: Baldwin II gives the Temple to Hugues de Payens and Godfrey de Saint Omer as the headquarters for their military order – thenceforth the 'Templars'.

TEMPLES AND TRUTH

IRONICALLY, the 'Temple' from which the Templars took their title was actually a Muslim monument, the Al-Aqsa Mosque. There's no evidence that it had ever been Solomon's Temple, as the Crusaders appear to have believed; nor that the next-door Dome of the Rock had been King Herod's 'Second Temple'.

Muhammad's *Mi'raj* had made the Temple Mount as holy for Muslims as for Jews or Christians: the site is eagerly visited (and hotly contested) to this day. Ecumenical despite themselves, the Crusaders embraced their misapprehension with immense enthusiasm. Celebrating modern mosques as ancient Jewish shrines, they then took them as the pattern for their churches. The circular plan of the Dome of the Rock (built atop the very outcrop from which the Prophet was held to have taken flight that fateful night) became the basis for the Templars' 'temple' churches both in the Holy Land and across Western Europe.

Below: What the Crusaders were convinced was King Solomon's Temple in Jerusalem appears actually to have been the al-Aqsa Mosque.

FIGHTING FOR FUNDS

The two orders were not exactly on level terms, though. Whether it was literally true or not, the story of De Payens' and De St Omer's shared horse reflected accurately enough the parlous position of the Knights Templar in the early years. The Order's first campaign, accordingly, wasn't a military one but a quasi-political, profile-building one; De Payens' first chivalric 'quest'

Below: The figure of Hugues de Payens takes on the exotic glamour of his Middle Eastern setting in Henri Lehmann's painting.

in Western Europe was a search for funds. Vital as Baldwin's gift had been in giving the Knights Templar a home, it left the building of the Order all to do.

In 1127, then, De Payens embarked on a protracted tour of the castle-courts of France, drumming up financial support for his great venture. By 1128, he had taken his message to Norman England. 'This same year', says the *Anglo-Saxon Chronicle*:

…came from Jerusalem Hugh of the Temple to the King in Normandy; and the King received him with much honour, and gave him rich presents in gold and in silver. And afterwards he sent him into England; and there he was received by all good men, who all gave him presents, and in Scotland also: and by him they sent to Jerusalem much wealth withal in gold and in silver.

Pious giving was well established, as we've seen, but a great many Middle East veterans (or just romantically minded armchair soldiers) found it more satisfying to donate to a cause combining spiritual purity with warlike glamour. Like the Hospitallers before them, the Knights Templar were to benefit from this instinct.

NETWORKING

THE 'nation state', historians tell us, is a comparatively modern phenomenon. Some scholars see it starting as recently as the nineteenth century. A medieval 'kingdom' – as its name suggests – centred power and identity on its monarch; its association with a country – with Scotland, say or France, was secondary and 'softer'. England's Angevin kings, for instance, ruled large territories in France through much of the twelfth and thirteenth centuries. Henry II (1133–89; reigned 1154-89) had actually been born in Le Mans, in the Loire region of northwestern France. His son and successor Richard I (1157–99; reigned 1189–99) was to die at Châlus, in Aquitaine, where he'd spent much of his later life.

At the same time, however, the idea of Christendom constituted a sort of cultural 'common market', offering an identity all west Europeans could share. (The rise of Islam had only reinforced this feeling.) It made perfect sense, then, for a man like Hugues de Payens to think in pan-European terms as he worked to build his order – first in his fundraising, but thereafter for ongoing administration too.

Hence the creation of up to ten provinces or *langues* – so-called because they were divided broadly along linguistic lines. Separate territories, then for England, France, Portugal, Apulia and Hungary in the west and Jerusalem, Antioch and Tripoli on the ground in the Middle East, each with its own autonomous Grand Priory and Master.

Below: Over time, the Templars' early poverty became emblematic. De Payens and Saint Omer share a horse in a statue in London's Temple Church.

In men as well as in money. De Payens' lobbying didn't just loosen old men's purse-strings: it fired already ardent and adventurous young men to enlist in his sacred cause. 'He invited folk out to Jerusalem,' the *Anglo-Saxon Chronicle* reports; 'and there went with him and after him more people than ever did before, since that the first expedition was in the day of Pope Urban'.

Not that the Order lost out financially in cases like this: it was customary for the aspiring monk from a wealthy family to bring an endowment with him when he joined a monastery, and so it was now with new recruits to the Knights Templar. It went without saying that young men like this, drawn exclusively from the aristocracy, tended to come from very wealthy homes. The author of the *Anglo-Saxon Chronicle*, indeed, went so far as to suggest that Sir Hugues was actually swindling his English hearers, persuading them to part with their sons and with enormous sums of money on the grounds that a great war with Islam was imminent, when at that time there was no such conflict to be fought.

CLEARLY NO
MILITARY-
MAN *MANQUÉ*,
BERNARD WAS
CARVING OUT
AN IMPORTANT
CAREER IN THE
CHURCH OF
HIS TIME AS AN
ADVOCATE
OF LARGE-SCALE
REFORM.

BERNARD'S BACKING

But if the old 'knightly' caste gave the new Knights Templar much of their support, they didn't go short of attention in more 'purely' ecclesiastical circles. They had a unique champion in St Bernard of Clairvaux. Not only did he help secure the Templars' recognition at the Council of Troyes (1129), he assisted in drawing up the Order's rule on behalf of Pope Honorius II (1060–1130; reigned 1124–30). He recorded his thinking on the subject after a few years of reflection in an influential treatise, *In Praise of the New Knighthood* (c. 1136).

Clearly no military-man *manqué*, Bernard was carving out an important career in the Church of his time as an advocate of large-scale – but wholly peaceable – reform. Even so, he shared the crusading dream, and had seen the logic in the letter De Payens brought with him from Baldwin II saying that what the Holy Land needed wasn't 'singing, wailing monks' but fighting men.

ABOVE THE LAW – BY LAW

THE KNIGHTS TEMPLAR's potential power was boosted immeasurably by a bull from Pope Innocent II (?–1143; reigned 1130–43). Entitled *Omne Datum Optimum* ('That all the Best Should be Given'), it basically allowed them to keep all the property they plundered and exempted them from the control of the local law wherever it might be.

As if this were not enough, Pope Celestine II (?–1144; in office 1143–4) followed up a few years later with *Milites Templi* ('Soldiers of the Temple', 1144). This accorded the Order the protection of the wider clergy and gave them sweeping powers to levy taxes and raise funds. His successor, Eugene III (c. 1080–1153; reigned 1145–53) brought out his own bull, *Militia Dei* ('God's Militia', 1145), guaranteeing the Templars' independence from the clergy and allowing them to build their own churches, take tithes (parish taxes) from their communities and charge burial fees.

Right: Pope Innocent II, from a manuscript illustration. He gave the Templars freedom to operate under the auspices of the Church.

Not that he didn't also anticipate spiritual benefits for the fighting men themselves. Even if peaceful prayer might be the ideal, it clearly wasn't for everyone. An order like De Payens',

Below: El Greco captures the compassion as well as the austerity of St Bernard of Clairvaux, an influential early advocate for the Knights Templar.

Bernard believed, was invaluable as a way of taking young noblemen's macho swagger usefully in hand and setting their aggression and intrepidness to work in the service of Our Lord.

SAINTLY SUPPORT

IN 1118, the year the Knights Templar were founded, it was also the year in which St Bernard (1090–1153) set up his first abbey. He was to revolutionize the monastic movement.

Founded by Robert de Molesme (1028–1111), the community at Cîteaux, near Dijon, northeastern France, was already striving to get back to Benedictine basics, but some young monks believed that the sheer scale and wealth of the great foundations militated against real humility and hard work.

So it was that in 1115, Bernard went off with a small party of like-minded brothers. At a hitherto-deserted spot at Clairvaux, in the Aube region, they established a new community, dedicated to a regime of work and prayer. A strict regime of worship was punctuated by spells of study and hard, productive manual work. In 1118, they felt emboldened enough to proclaim their existence as a new order, named the 'Cistercians' in honour of their parent-house, Cîteaux.

If the Cistercian programme sounds in all essentials much the same as St Benedict's

Above: St Bernard and his Cistercians set up their new foundation at Clairvaux (1118), an important monastic centre from that time on.

'Rule', that's no coincidence: it was a conscious attempt to take monasticism back to its roots. So rich had so many foundations grown, between their own efforts in agriculture and industry and the pious endowments that kept pouring in, that they appeared to have left all humility behind.

Bernard was to be an important inspiration and an influential ally for the Knights Templar, and his spiritual thinking is strongly evident in their 'rule'.

Opposite: The secrecy
surrounding the Templars'
initiation ceremony
inevitably prompted
rumours that grew
extravagant: denying
Christ's divinity; trampling
the crucifix…

THE RULE A
KNIGHT FOLLOWED
WAS A CURIOUS
AMALGAM OF
THE CHIVALRIC
AND THE
BENEDICTINE
CODES.

Both the Knights Templar and Knights Hospitaller were knights before they were monks. They had to be, really: knighthood was its own institution, with its own rules and its own procedures. The applicant to either Order had to be a knight – officially 'dubbed' – before he joined. The rule he then followed was a curious amalgam of the chivalric and the Benedictine codes.

We know more about the Rule the Templars followed – though it seems unlikely that the Hospitallers' was very different. First and foremost, the Templar Rule stipulated, the knight who wished to join the Order had to agree to 'renounce [his] own will' – which, extreme as it may seem, makes clear sense in both monastic and military terms. Just as the monk must suppress his sense of self for the good of his community, and submit to the direction of his abbot, so the soldier has to submit to his commanders.

In this case, the chain of command was held to come down through the Church hierarchy, so ultimately from the Pope – hence the echo of Christ's words to Peter in the Knights Templar's Rule:

When anything shall be ordered by the Master, there must be no hesitation: it shall be done with no delay, as though it had been ordered by heaven.

PROHIBITIONS

The Knight Templar was to be a 'knight-at-arms': he wasn't to be a knight at leisure. Sports such as hunting and falconry were to be left behind by the postulant on joining the Order, for example. So were other customs of the court. Hair was not to be worn long, of course: the tonsure of the monk was conventionally adopted. Military practicality and religious humility met in this stipulation.

Fine, fashionable clothing was obviously out. Plain robes were worn. In the field of battle, it was much the same. Other knights might brandish ornate swords and maces and richly-decorated shields with their own identifying insignia on them, but not the Knights Templar. Other knights might go peacocking off to war in richly ornamented armour and brightly-coloured heraldic surcoats, but not the Templars. They wore a blank, white mantle

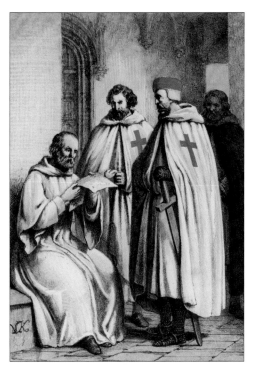

Above: The Templars' plain white robes represented the moral purity they aspired to and the simplicity in which they sought to live their lives.

that implicitly proclaimed their purity and their freedom from all vanity. (Though it goes without saying that they wore it with the utmost pride!)

Also off-limits were the wit and elegance of courtly conversation: Knights Templar were to speak as little as possible, and then 'decently and humbly, without laughter'. Talking too much was in itself a sin, as a pointer to personal vanity. Listening was a much more worthwhile occupation. Mealtimes were as meticulously scheduled as services of worship – and as strictly policed. They weren't social gatherings, but religious rituals in themselves.

THE TEMPLAR AND THE TEMPTRESS

Celibacy was strictly enforced as we've seen; as a rigid requirement it was relatively new. Chivalric convention might ordain that the knight should be a devoted servant to and protector of the fair, but femininity and the wiles of women were to be feared. They were, the Rule reminded them, a well-established weapon of the 'ancient Enemy' – the Devil – who had:

…led many from the straight path to paradise through the society of women. Heretofore, dearest brothers, that the flower of chastity be always maintained among you, let this custom be dispensed with from now on.

Just in case the message hadn't got through, the drafters of the Rule returned to it in its conclusion (a modern psychologist might sense a certain anxiety here). 'Lastly,' they said, summing up their code:

…we hold it dangerous for all religious to gaze too much on the countenances of women; and therefore no brother shall presume to kiss neither widow, nor virgin, nor mother, nor sister, nor aunt, nor any other woman. Let the Knighthood of Christ shun feminine kisses through which men have very often been drawn into danger, so that each, with a pure conscience, may be able to walk everlastingly in the sight of God.

INITIAL INITIATION

Great play was later to be made of the elaborate secrecy surrounding initiation into the Knights Templar. In good times – during the decades of their rise – this would serve them well by boosting their mystique; later, though, it would stir extravagant suspicion. To begin with, at any rate, the indications are that the ceremony was brief and simple.

Chastity was again given emphasis when the postulant (the candidate for joining the Order) knelt at the Grand Master's feet to make the vows that would finally confirm him as a member. He wore a length of rope around his waist, to signal that his body was cordoned off from sexual contact.

But this was just one aspect of a general renunciation of selfhood he was promising to make in return for membership of the Order. 'Good brother,' the Master apparently told him:

Below: François-Marius Granet's atmospheric account of Jacques de Molay's initiation. He was to be the last Grand Master of the Templars.

You ask a very great thing, for you now see only the outside of our Order. Superficially, it may be seen that we have fine horses and harness, and that we eat and drink well and are provided with clothing and you might easily imagine that you will be at your ease with us. You cannot, however, appreciate the strictness of the rule we have to follow. Most of all, it is hard for a young man like you, who have the privilege of being master to yourself, willingly to make yourself someone else's serf.

Placing his hands on a Bible, then, the young man swore to obey his superiors in the Order, to fight to the death for the Holy Land and to sustain himself in poverty, chastity and obedience. In particular, he promised to shun simony, and sodomy, on pain of lifelong imprisonment.

Right: In Dante's *Inferno* (imagined here by Gustave Doré), Simonists are buried upside-down, in keeping with the way they inverted the moral order.

Nor, he pledged, would he reveal the Order's secrets. This, of course, was to be the vow that really pricked the critics' curiosity. We've no reason to think that the Knights Templar actually *had* any seriously-significant secrets in these their early years – a general confidentiality would have been all that was required. In later centuries, however, as their power and wealth expanded and, with these things, the concerns that were coming to surround the Order, interest in their 'secrets' grew and grew.

KNIGHTS OF ST LAZARUS

AT AROUND THE SAME time as the Knights Templar – in around 1118–19 – another military order was founded; this one by the carers at one of Jerusalem's biggest monastic leper hospitals. Hence its name, the Order of St Lazarus. The poor man 'covered with sores' who in Jesus' famous parable (Luke 16, 19–31) lay spurned and unassisted outside Dives' gate, only to find salvation in the rich man's stead, Lazarus had become the patron saint of lepers.

The Knights of St Lazarus achieved royal recognition from King Fulk of Jerusalem in 1142, though it was not to be till 1255 that they were acknowledged as an order by Pope Alexander IV (c. 1185–1261; reigned 1254–61). They had founded a number of hospitals for lepers in that time. While recruits into the Order's fighting

force were to begin with drawn from the hospital carers, patients were soon joining up as well. By the middle of the twelfth century, of course, they had the inspirational example of Baldwin IV: leprosy didn't have to be a bar to heroism, he'd shown.

Not too much is known of the Order's actual battle honours, though they are known to have played a part in the defence of Acre in the years leading up to its (for the Crusaders) calamitous siege of 1291. After that city's fall, the Order set up in Cyprus, from where they extended a chain of hospitals into mainland Europe. The Knights of St Lazarus still survive, and still carry out charitable works, though their chivalric status is largely ceremonial these days.

Left: A Knight of St Lazarus.

The Templars' daily regimen was tough – though not noticeably more so than that of more monastic orders. There were indeed clear resemblances between the two ways of life. The Knights Templar certainly seem to have followed much the same horarium as was laid down in the Benedictine Rule.

The main differences were that they spent the time after Matins tending to their horses rather than snatching a few hours' further sleep, and that their study and work time went on military training. On campaign, of course, this timetable had to be relaxed to some extent. Even so, as far as practicable, a comparatively strict regime of prayer and worship was maintained. It seems likely that the Knights Hospitaller had a similar regime.

HEAVY CAVALRY

From a tactical point of view, as knights, the Templars and Hospitallers were what we'd now class as 'heavy cavalry'. They served as shock troops – as the Templars were to at Montgisard. This meant that they generally needed to be backed by more lightly-armed turcopoles and foot soldiers (who in turn needed sergeants to keep them in order).

These, though loosely attached to the Order, weren't entitled by rank or background to be knights – nor, however, were they bound by the same sort of religious vows or disciplines as the Knights Templar or Hospitaller. Laymen also seem to have been hired to serve in specialist roles like that of castellan (running fortresses), for example.

Right: A Crusader kneels in prayer, prior to going into battle. Faith and fighting went together for the military orders.

FLYING THE FLAG

THE KNIGHTS TEMPLAR RODE into battle beneath a black-and-white banner – the white was for their pious purity, of course. The black represented the doom they were going to mete out to the enemies of Christ. The white field might additionally be marked out with a red cross in what would come to be known as the 'Maltese' style, on account of that island's close connections with the Order in later centuries.

On the Hospitallers' flag, less familiar now, a straight white cross stood out against a bright red background. It too has modern Maltese connections, remaining in use by the Sovereign Military Order of Malta – a slightly mysterious Catholic lay-order which traces its history back to the Knights Hospitaller and concerns itself with charitable works.

A NEW CRUSADE

'True believers, fight against the infidels who are near you, and be hard on them.' So says an inscription left by Hisham I (757–96; reigned 788–96) in the Great Mosque of Córdoba. The Islamic ruler's sentiments were of course exactly mirrored in the hearts of those Christian rulers who still held something like sway in Iberia – for the most part in the north.

Islamic invaders had been streaming across the Straits of Gibraltar since the end of the seventh century: they'd even made it into France before being held at Poitiers (732). Over the centuries that followed, the identity of Spain was to be forged in fighting: the *Reconquista* – the 'reconquest' of those territories taken by the Moors – became the guiding project of the nation. At least it did in retrospect. Ultimately, these wars were to become the stuff of legend, a patriotic 'founding myth', though the reality was much more messy and confused.

Only gradually did the *Reconquista* take on the character of a crusade – a continuation of the struggle taking place in the Middle East. It had begun much earlier, for one thing; for another, it had started as a frantic fight for survival and gradually assumed the additional character of an intra-Christian power

SLOWLY AND
PAINFULLY, THE
CHRISTIANS
WERE CLAWING
BACK WHAT THEY
BELIEVED TO BE
THEIRS.

struggle. By the middle of the eighth century, the Moors had occupied almost the entire Iberian Peninsula. The only conquests here were going to the forces of Islam.

There had been hopeful signs, however. In 722, amid the mountains of Asturias, they had been held by the local Visigothic ruler, Pelayo (c. 685–737; reigned 718–37), at the Battle of Covadonga. Here, at least, the idea of a Christian Spain had endured.

Asturias hadn't just survived, but over the period that followed had actually extended its boundaries. In 910, indeed, it had been divided into two. A new kingdom – Galicia – was established in the west, while a new state was centred on León. Next door, the Kingdom of Castile was created: in the eleventh century these two were to be united as the Kingdom of Castile and León. Further east, meanwhile, in the wake of Frankish incursions across the Pyrenees, the kingdoms of Navarra, Aragón and Catalunya all emerged. The whole of northern Spain was now in Christian hands, even if it was a patchwork of little states that warred as much with one another as with the Moors.

Slowly and painfully, though, the Christians were clawing back what they believed was theirs, even if as of 1100 the whole of Andalusía and Valencia, and southern Portugal, remained in Moorish hands. In around 1145, the Order of Calatrava was formed at the castle of Calatrava la Vieja, north of Ciudad Real in Castile-La Mancha. It was named for those knights with whose valorous support King Alfonso VII (1105–57; reigned 1126–57) had seized this strategic fortress from the Moors.

In the years that followed, the Order of Calatrava was to win important victories – and be richly rewarded with grants of land and treasure by the crowns of Castile and León and Aragón. Like the Knights Hospitaller and Templar, albeit on a much more local basis, it was building its own network of connections, power and wealth.

PRIDE OF PORTUGAL

In 1146, just a year after the creation of the Order of Calatrava, a group of knights in Portugal established their own military

order to fight the might of Islam. Like that of Calatrava, the Order of Aviz was named for an important citadel seized from the Moors. When, in 1162, they adopted their own version of the Benedictine Rule to govern their daily life, they became known as the Knights of St Benedict of Aviz.

Their status was quickly recognized by King Afonso I (c. 1106–85; reigned 1139–85) – not just the first Afonso, but the first king of Portugal. And, in fact, the founder of the country. He'd set the state up himself, in rebellion against the rulers of Castile and León, and saw the Order as essential to its patriotic pride. He made his illegitimate half-brother, Pedro Henriques, its first Grand Master.

Anxious to see their wealth and prestige grow, Afonso presented the Knights with all the lands and rents of Évora when that town was taken from the Moors in 1166. From that time on, accordingly, its members were also to have the title of the Friars of Santa María de Évora.

Right: Afonso I founded Portugal in opposition both to Islamic and to Castilian Spanish rule.

3

HOLY WAR, UNHOLY SHAMBLES

The military orders shared in the dismal series of setbacks the Crusaders now endured in the Middle East. But what didn't quite kill them seems to have made them strong.

EANWHILE, in the Middle East, the Crusader kingdoms were reeling from the loss of the County of Edessa to Zengi's Islamic army. The Turkish *atabeg* (or governor) of Mosul, in what's now Iraq, Imad ad-Din Zengi (c. 1085–1146; reigned 1127–46) had seen off several rivals in the Saracen camp to make himself master of Aleppo, Homs and Hama too. In 1144, he turned his attentions to those infidel forces were in the Middle East as occupiers. The city of Edessa fell after a four-month siege: a deep humiliation to the royal and ecclesiastical elites of Christian Europe – and the immediate spur to a Second Crusade.

AVENGING EDESSA
Like the First Crusade, the Second was set in motion by a papal plea – this time that of Eugene III. Like his mentor, St Bernard of

Opposite: As imagined by Gustave Doré in the nineteenth century, Knight Templar Jacques de Maille dies a heroic death during the Second Crusade.

Clairvaux, he was personally a man of peace, but had immense enthusiasm for the crusading ideal. St Bernard, it was widely reported, while respecting his protegé's sincerity, thought him wholly unsuited to the responsibility and dignity of Pope. Even so, he threw his spiritual weight behind Pope Eugene III's new venture.

At Easter 1146, thousands thronged to Vézelay, Burgundy, to hear this 'honey-tongued teacher' preach. His sermon had the same effect as Urban's fifty years before. Bernard travelled through much of Europe issuing his call to Christian arms: wherever he went, there were scenes of mass hysteria. On 27 December 1146, he addressed the Assembly at Speyer with such conviction that King Conrad III of Germany (1093–1152; reigned 1138–52) enlisted on the spot.

France's King Louis VII (1120–80; reigned 1137–80) was bound by guilt to respond to his pontiff's call. In 1142, he'd

Below: St Bernard stirs up enthusiasm for the Second Crusade.

gone to war with Count Theobald II of Champagne (1090–52; reigned 1137–52) in defiance of Eugene's predecessor, Innocent II. To add injury to insult, he'd conducted a cruel siege of Vitry-le-François, burning down a church tower inside which a thousand civilians had taken refuge. As blasphemous as it was bloody, Louis' crime cried out to heaven for vengeance – he seems to have felt so himself. St Bernard's words at Vézelay served only to convince him further: this Second Crusade would be his chance to make things right.

A FATEFUL MEETING

Above: Pope Eugene, Louis VII and the French Templars meet in Paris to plan the Second Crusade.

IN APRIL 1147, Pope Eugene and King Louis VII came together in person to the Paris Temple to discuss the up-coming campaign with Everard des Barres (?–1174; in office 1147–51), the French Grand Master, and his men. The Knights Templar, it was agreed, were to take a leading role. It seems to have been in honour of this agreement that the Pope gave them the right to adorn their plain, white mantles with the famous bright red cross we tend to associate today with the crusading knights at large.

Not to be outdone, King Louis bestowed on the Order the right to collect and handle the taxes he'd levied to help fund the Crusade, giving the Knights an important 'in' at the French treasury. (Over time, their hold on the finances of France was only to strengthen – in the end, alarmingly. Paranoia about the Order would grow as this influence did.)

It was further agreed that Des Barres would take charge of negotiations with the Byzantine emperor, Manuel I Komnenos (1118–80; reigned 1143–80), over the use of Constantinople as a staging post.

CRUSADING CARVE-UP

Conrad's contingent, ready before the French, set off overland from Constantinople but suffered a shattering defeat at Dorylaeum, southern Turkey, in 1147. What was left of Conrad's army met up with Louis', which, coming to Ephesus by sea, had now landed safely but still faced a difficult journey across mountainous country to reach the Holy Land. Their heavily armoured knights and their sluggish infantry, slowed down by the rugged terrain, were an easy target for the light cavalry of the Seljuk Turks.

With Louis' army in desperate straits, the Knights Templar saved the day – though only to the extent of damage reduction.

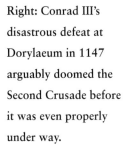

Right: Conrad III's disastrous defeat at Dorylaeum in 1147 arguably doomed the Second Crusade before it was even properly under way.

Still, preserving the whole French force from annihilation was in its way a triumph. Everard broke the army up into smaller detachments, each one led by a troop of Templars who, by sheer will and brutal force, powered their charges through to safety at Antalya at the southern coast.

This, of course, still left them some way short of their destination. For a few, there were eventually places on the ships of a Byzantine fleet sent to their rescue; the rest faced a further route march, in the course of which they mostly perished.

It was, then, a much-reduced (and deeply demoralized) force that finally made it to the Holy Land. And, after all that, bickering between the new arrivals and the established Crusaders in the region fatally compromised their collective mission. The Siege of Damascus (July 1148) broke down in disarray, the Crusaders being worn down within a matter of days by the baking heat and waterless conditions in the desert surrounding the city before their blockade could even begin to 'bite'. Further losses were sustained during an ignominious retreat.

Above: The War Council at Acre (1148) set in motion the Siege of Damascus. This is a lovely depiction of what was to be a grim defeat.

The consequences were far-reaching. If the Second Crusade had come to nothing, the Kingdom of Jerusalem, whose leadership had proposed and directed the catastrophic siege, had lost its credibility just about completely. Certainly that was how William of Tyre saw it. One of Jerusalem's leading churchmen (and, of course, the tutor to Baldwin IV), William's loyalty to the

Opposite: Baldwin III, as represented in stained glass in the Basilica of Holy Blood in Bruges, Belgium.

Kingdom was unquestioning, but he felt its authority had been badly damaged here. Europe's Christian heroes had been let down:

A company of kings and princes such as we have not read of through all the ages had gathered and, for our sins, had been forced to return, covered with shame and disgrace, with their mission unfulfilled.

Although the modern reader might be slower than William to blame the 'sins' of Jerusalem for the Damascus disaster, the Kingdom clearly hadn't covered itself with glory. 'Henceforth, so long as they remained in the East,' William reports, the European Crusaders 'regarded the ways of our princes with suspicion'. They were wary and deeply sceptical of all their plans.

Even after they had returned to their own lands they constantly remembered the injuries they had suffered and detested our princes as wicked men.

The whole crusading ideal had been compromised, it seems.

They also caused others who had not been there to neglect the care of the kingdom, so that henceforth those who undertook the pilgrimages were fewer and less fervent.

THE WHOLE CRUSADING IDEAL HAD BEEN COMPROMISED, IT SEEMS.

ON THE DEFENSIVE, ON THE UP

A depressed Des Barres returned to France, to a life of quiet contemplation and prayer, which in any case came to an end a few years later. His men remained in the Holy Land where, with the Hospitallers, they were placed in charge of policing the borders of the *Outremer* (literally 'Beyond the Sea'), as the Crusader states collectively were known.

The Templars built several castles to this end. In the north they made a rebuilt Byzantine fort at Bagras, in the Amanus Mountains, the central point for a long and strong defensive line. Likewise, in the south, they strengthened a castle built by Baldwin III (1130–63; reigned 1143–63) a few years earlier to keep back Islamic forces based in Egypt. The Hospitallers too were digging in – most notably at Crac des Chevaliers, the most celebrated 'Crusader castle' of them all.

A quiet period, on the face of it, then, but behind the apparent uneventfulness there's another story, of economic ascendancy,

MOTHER KNOWS BEST

BY THE EARLY 1150s, the Kingdom of Jerusalem was spiralling into civil war, which broke out in earnest in 1152. The struggle was basically over who was to be the boss between Baldwin III and his mother Melisende (1105–61).

Baldwin being just an infant when his grandfather, Baldwin II had died in 1131, the succession had passed to Melisende's husband (so Baldwin II's son-in-law), King Fulk. Actually, that's not quite true – or at least not the whole story. Melisende, a cheerfully single woman, had been in Baldwin II's eyes (and, emphatically, in her own) the old man's intended successor, but it had been thought fitting that she should be wed. Hence the match with Fulk – though even then, her father seems to have been so keen for Melisende to wield authority that before he died he had her made sole guardian of her son with Fulk. Their marriage appears to have been one of opportunity on both sides; and soon to have degenerated into one of power struggle.

Fulk won out, and has indeed been acknowledged by history as an important and largely successful ruler. The Kingdom of Jerusalem was arguably at its strongest during his reign. By the time he died in 1143, Baldwin III was thirteen – his nephew Baldwin IV was actually to reign at that age. But his mother, appointed regent, grasped at power with both hands, and then refused to give it up. A decade later,

well into his majority, Baldwin III was reduced to going to war with Melisende to assert his rightful authority over his realm.

It was a bitter dispute, but as soon as it was over, Baldwin made sure that Melisende remained at his side as the closest of his counsellors. Whatever their mother–son issues, he knew better than to dispense with her experience and intelligence. Mother knew best....

to be traced. The construction of fortifications on such a scale was fiscally far beyond the Crusader states. But the Knights Hospitaller and Templar were backed by the resources they already commanded, thanks to their landholdings here and back in Europe, while contributions continued to pour in from pious donors. They were, accordingly, able to step into this financial breach. They also reaped the rewards: in building these castles, they were building less tangible empires of influence, prestige and power.

Throughout this period, in fact, we see behind a headline-history of humiliations, setbacks and defeats, a *relative* improvement in the position of the military orders. The Second Crusade might have been an abject failure, but the Knights Templar had been there when it counted in the mountains, saving Louis' army – and *not* been there when key decisions had been taken at Damascus. Again and again, missteps by the monarchical authorities played into the military orders' hands. Civil war within the Kingdom of Jerusalem (see box) only strengthened them still further.

'KEY TO THE CHRISTIAN LANDS': CRAC DES CHEVALIERS

JUST ABOUT EVERYONE's mental image of a medieval castle, this impressive pile atop a rugged outcrop in the Syrian desert, inland from Tartus, was occupied by the Knights Hospitaller for centuries. It was consequently known as *Crac* (probably from the Arabic *karak*, or 'fort') *de l'Ospital*. But romantically-minded nineteenth-century historians couldn't see this as a credibly warlike handle – hence its modern name.

Its magnificence and formidable strength were in keeping with the castle's strategic significance, overlooking as it did the main route between Tripoli and Homs. It was big enough to accommodate not only 2000 defenders but sufficient food to keep them going for two years. The Hospitallers substantially rebuilt the castle, which became (in the words of Hungary's King Andrew II (c. 1177–1235; reigned 1205–35) 'the key to the Christian lands'.

As such, it was often to find itself in the thick of the fighting until the final failure of the crusading movement towards the end of the thirteenth century. Unfortunately, it's found itself swept up in a much more modern conflict, too, sustaining serious damage in the recent Syrian Civil War.

This unearned political dividend didn't escape the notice of contemporary commentators – hence William of Tyre's resentful carpings against the Templars. Be that as it might, the continuing lack of certainty at the centre of Crusader society on the ground in the Middle East could only give their relative importance an important boost.

EXPLOITING THE ASSASSINS

The Templars found other, stranger sources of income and prestige – as when they took upon themselves the duty of avenging Raymond II, Count of Tripoli. A generous donor to the military orders, Raymond had in 1149 given the Knights Templar the castle of Araima.

In 1152, the Count was assassinated by the original 'assassins'. The *Hashashin* were a secretive Shia sect, whose doctrines included certain pre-Islamic elements (they were said to use hashish in their more mystic rituals). But it was to be their militants' policy of picking off enemy leaders in targeted killings that was to be the basis of their historic notoriety, and to lead to

Below: The iconic Crusader Castle: Crac des Chevaliers, outside Tartus, Syria, saw bloody action many times in the medieval era.

Below: A group of
Hashashin receive
instruction from their
leader, the mysterious 'Old
Man of the Mountain',
Rashid ad-Din Sinan.

our modern usage of their name. The *Hashashin's* list of enemies
in fact included a great many Muslims – Sunni divines. But
Raymond, a ruthless scourge of their communities in Tripoli,
and around its borders, certainly qualified.

The Templars responded to his murder by hunting the
Hashashin's ringleaders down and levying a hefty annual
tribute – essentially protection money.

ASCALON UNDER SIEGE

Under Des Barres' successor Bernard de Tremelay (?–1153; in
office 1149–53), this defensive posture was for the most part to
be maintained. Not that more aggressive initiatives weren't taken:
the Crusaders' greatest triumph of this time was to come from
one of these at the southern frontier fortress-city of Ascalon, in
1153. De Tremelay's Templars were of course to play their part.

Formidably fortified and resolutely guarded, Ascalon had
seen off one siege already, in 1148, attacked by Conrad III in the

THE FADING FATIMIDS

IF THE SECOND CRUSADE had ended badly, foundering in ghastly farce, there were problems on the Saracen side as well. Western historiography has seen Zengi's capture of Edessa as above all a crushing defeat for the Crusaders – and rightly so. But it was also the culmination of Imad ad-Din Zengi's rise, after many years of intra-Islamic faction-fighting. In the Muslim world, as in the Christian, leaders and dynasties rose and fell – as the Fatimids were doing now in Egypt.

They'd achieved their ascendancy – and in no uncertain terms – in the early decades of the tenth century, when Abdullah al-Mahdi Billah (873–934; reigned 909–34) had carved out a caliphate in North Africa.

Called the Fatimids on account of their supposed descent from Fatima, the Prophet's beloved daughter, they had dominated the Islamic world with an empire extending from what is now Morocco to Egypt's Red Sea coast and established a big and impressive capital in Cairo.

Their adherence to a slightly off-beat Ismaili Shia religious

movement had marked them out from other Islamic rulers. But it hadn't been until the reign of the sixth Caliph, Al-Hakim bi-Amr Allah (985–1021; reigned 996–1021) that the empire would experience the puritanical potential of this movement in its full repressive force.

Al-Hakim left behind him a divided and a badly weakened caliphate, though under his successors the Fatimid Dynasty limped along. Its power and authority were gradually crumbling, though. At the time of the First Crusade, in 1099, a Fatimid army sent to assist in the defence of Jerusalem had been stopped by Crusaders at Ascalon; now the city was to be the scene of a second Christian triumph.

Top: Two Fatimid warriors, from an ink drawing of the eleventh century.

Left: The Fatimid Caliph, Al-Hakim bi-Amr Allah.

course of the Second Crusade. The Fatimids were in no doubt of the city's importance: an important commercial centre, it was also strategically vital, controlling overland access to Egypt from the east.

In January 1153, accordingly, King Baldwin's army found it well-defended. 'In addition to its walls and barbicans, its towers and ramparts', writes William of Tyre:

The city was supplied with arms and provisions beyond all expectation and it had an experienced population accustomed to the use of arms. There were so many of them that from the beginning of the siege to its end the numbers of the besieged were double those of the besiegers.

Below: The Siege of Ascalon, as imagined in an illumination by the fifteenth-century French artist Jean Colombe.

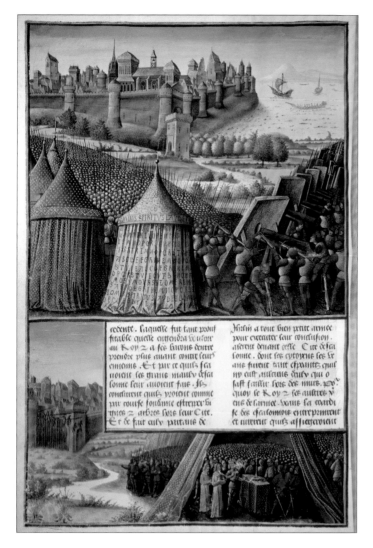

Emboldened by this strength, the garrison sent out parties at night to attack the Crusaders in their tents, leaving them confused as to who exactly was under siege. They laboured long days building colossal siege-engines to attack the city walls, only to see them destroyed in a matter of minutes, burned down by the defenders as quickly as they could be deployed.

Another crusading calamity in the making? It was certainly starting to look that way as the months went by with no sign of the city's defences so much as cracking. The Christians' ships, anchored offshore, were quickly chased away by the Fatimid fleet, leaving them further exposed and beleaguered, while the city was restocked with fresh supplies.

Week in, week out, though, the blockade had been taking its toll. Ascalon's big garrison may have been a source of strength, but it took a lot of feeding. Psychologically too, for those inside, the unexpected resilience of the Crusaders was difficult to take. They might have been discouraged by their setbacks but they were nevertheless still there.

Easter brought a new influx of Christian pilgrims to the Holy Land: many of them chose to stay on and fight for their faith at Ascalon. This was a new lease of life for the siege, and, conversely, a dampener for the city's defenders who'd been hoping to see the prospect of an end by now.

The stalemate was stressful for both sides, of course. If Fatimid forces were disappointed to see so many enemy reinforcements suddenly appearing, the Crusaders were cast down when, despite this, no breakthrough came. With no material sign of progress either way, psychology was crucial. By August, after seven months' siege, King Baldwin was about to throw in his hand. Contemporary sources suggest that he was talked out of this decision by a group of Knights Hospitaller, there with the Order's master, the impressively-named Raymond du Puy de Provence (1083–1160; in office c. 1121–60). He still had everything to play for, they urged the king.

CONTENTIOUS COURAGE

The Hospitallers appear to have been at Ascalon in a wholly advisory capacity – vital as their advice turned out to be – but the Knights Templar were to play a much more active role. They were, accounts of the time agree, the first to advance when, at the siege's end, the first narrow breach appeared in the city walls, a small group forcing its way in through a hail of arrows, bolts and other missiles.

As one contemporary chronicler puts it, in his account of the overthrow of this heathen 'Babylon':

The chief leader and commander of that army, which serves from the Temple under the profession of fraternal fellowship, rushed in with his troop, and, reaching an open space in the city

Above: Raymond du Puy de Provence, Grand Master of the Hospitallers, c. 1121–60, played a decisive role at the Siege of Ascalon.

surrounded by his band of men, he established a position; there, limited by the narrowness of the streets, closed in by walls and the overhanging roofs of the buildings.

A courageous move, undoubtedly, but Tremelay had exposed his force to dreadful danger:

beset from every side by a growing crowd, he was overwhelmed and slain with the entire body of his men. The heads of whom were gathered in one heap so they might be displayed to the king of Babylon as a sign of victory; they hung the bodies on the walls, taunting us and provoking the army of God with words of blasphemy.

A heroic action? Not if we're to believe William of Tyre's version. In his view, the Templars stood their ground in the gap in the walls only to prevent others entering and sharing their order's glory – and their plunder. William couldn't even bring himself to sympathize with the situation of those cut down and mutilated – in their greed and vanity they'd provided the defenders with important trophies, rekindling their courage and giving them a means of messing with the morale of the Crusaders.

Notwithstanding these reservations, the reality is that the siege was all but over now. Wave after wave of Christian attackers hurled themselves into the gap the Templars had left.

Ascalon had fallen: this was a triumph of the sort that the Crusaders didn't have too many of. For most, despite William, it was a cause of great rejoicing.

WAVE AFTER WAVE OF CHRISTIAN ATTACKERS HURLED THEMSELVES INTO THE GAP THE TEMPLARS HAD LEFT.

Left: Baldwin III receives the homage of Ascalon's Saracen commanders after the successful conclusion of the city's siege.

BLOOD MONEY

Above: With its distinctive architecture – and the Templars' emblem atop its column outside – the Temple Church remains a London landmark to this day.

St Thomas of Canterbury, or Thomas Becket (c. 1119–70; in office 1162–70) was one of medieval England's most celebrated saints. It was to his shrine that Chaucer's Canterbury Pilgrims were to make their way in the *Canterbury Tales*.

His murder was notoriously – if, it seems, unknowingly (he cried out 'Who will rid me of this turbulent priest!', and loyal courtiers did the rest) – ordered by King Henry II (1133–89; reigned 1154–89). It rocked the Christian world, and left Henry prostrated with guilt.

As part of his penance, Henry agreed to pay for the upkeep of 200 Templar knights in the Holy Land. He also seems to have taken a (quite voluntary) interest in the Order's activities in England. By 1185, the Order's English Master was sitting in the House of Lords as *Primus Baro* – 'First Baron' – of the Kingdom. That same year saw a new headquarters consecrated for them in London's Temple Church. Henry is believed to have been in the congregation.

The Temple Church was round in plan, and like most Templar churches, modelled on (what they believed to have been) the 'real' Temple – Jerusalem's Dome of the Rock. A more regular rectangular chancel was added in the thirteenth century.

BEFORE A FALL

Under Baldwin's younger brother Amalric (1136–74; reigned 1168–74), Jerusalem enjoyed further victories over Fatimid Egypt, badly weakened by political division now. The military orders made hay. The contemporary chronicler Lambert de Wattrelos described one attack (in 1168) on Bilbeis, a city just south of the Nile Delta:

Above: King Amalric of Jerusalem meets the Emperor Manuel I Komemnos. The King had hopes of recovering Antioch from the Byzantines.

The Lord of the Hospital of Jerusalem went on the campaign with his men. He was sharp and confident in his prowess as a warrior, strong and intrepid in the fray. At last he arrived, with God's assistance, at a formidably fortified city named Bilbeis. The prince didn't fear the strength or courage of its people but boldly threw himself and his men forward at the city. They quickly breached the walls and levelled the place within, putting those who sought to stop them to the sword.

The 'Lord of the Hospital', Gilbert d'Assailly (?–1183; in office 1163–70), might have done better to have been a little less audacious. One triumphant raid does not a successful invasion make. Weak though the Fatimids might have been, Egypt was too vast and formidable a territory for them to think of conquering. The expedition petered out, leaving the Kingdom of Jerusalem humiliated and the Knights Hospitaller bankrupt.

Not only was D'Assailly forced to resign: the Order was censured by Pope Alexander III (c. 1100–81; reigned 1159–81). He considered that an adventure like the invasion of Egypt stretched beyond breaking-point the Hospitallers' already very wide interpretation of their remit to help the sick and protect pilgrims. Even so, all indications are that, once back on its feet financially, the Order let a decent period elapse but then resumed its raiding activities, if rather more discreetly.

NORTHERN OFFENSIVE

To the north, in Syria, meanwhile, the *atabeg* of Aleppo, Nur ud-Din (1118–74; reigned 1146–74 in Aleppo, 1156–74 in Damascus) was on the rise, an influential successor to Imad ad-Din Zengi. He'd already resisted attempts by crusading forces to retake Edessa and, in 1149, at Inab, Syria, inflicted a damaging defeat on Antioch's Christian ruler Prince Raymond of Poitiers (c. 1115–49; reigned 1136–49).

Since that time, by a judicious programme of alliance-building, he'd made himself the leader of the Muslims in the Middle East, and a formidable foe to the Crusaders. Nur ud-Din's calls for *jihad* against the western infidels inspired a generation of young Muslim warriors. Unfortunately for him, he wasn't destined to see this through.

Not that he didn't make a most promising start, in 1157 besieging the Knights Hospitaller in their castle at Banias, in the Golan Heights. That siege was broken, by Baldwin III and his army, but not before Nur ud-Din had dented the Templars' pride, capturing their Grand Master Bertrand de Blanquefort (c. 1109–69; in office 1156–69). After being held prisoner for three years, he was handed over to the Byzantines, who'd made an accommodation with the Turkish leader.

Below: A work of wishful thinking more than of historical exactitude, perhaps: an indignant-looking Nur ud-Din is put to flight.

Nur ud-Din's own days were numbered, though. His campaign to expel the infidel from the Middle East was cruelly cut short by his death from a fever in 1174. His son – and at least his nominal successor – As-Salih Ismail al-Malik (1163–81) was only eleven, so Nur ud-Din's realms were placed under the regency of his widow, As-Salih Ismail's mother, Ismat ud-Din Khatun (?–1186).

SALADIN: SELF-MADE SULTAN

All the indications are that Ismat ud-Din Khatun made a strong and competent leader. For William of Tyre, she had 'courage beyond that of most women'. Among those generals who flocked

to show her fealty was Salah ud-Din or Saladin, who made such an impression that, two years later, she married him. He was, indeed, a formidable figure: not yet forty, he had already made himself the master of Egypt (where Fatimid authority now existed only in name) and was already cutting a swathe through Syria.

Born in Tikrit, Iraq, of Kurdish ancestry, he found his way into the Seljuks' service through his uncle Asad ud-Din Shirkuh (?–1169), an important general for Nur ud-Din. Saladin had accompanied

Above: Saladin, as seen (it's believed) by his contemporary: the celebrated artist, inventor and engineer Ismail al-Jazari (1136–1206).

him during the campaigns of conquest he'd conducted in Egypt on Nur ud-Din's behalf. Saladin's dash and flair facilitated his rapid rise. In marrying Ismat, while she gained a strongman to secure her status, he forged a quasi-dynastic connection with Nur ud-Din and won a ready-made powerbase in Damascus. At the Battle of the Horns of Hama (1175; the 'horns' were a distinctly shaped hill outside the Syrian city), he put the supporters of Zengi's sons to flight. His victory here left his power and authority undisputed across the Middle East as Sultan of Egypt and Syria.

Across the *Muslim* Middle East, that is. For, all too obviously, there was a ragged hole at the heart of his empire where the Crusaders had their kingdom. It rankled the more that this

included Jerusalem's sacred mount. Saladin's wish to sweep the infidels away was entirely understandable – and only grew more bitter after his humiliation at Montgisard, 1177.

Above: Ascalon, taken at such cost only three decades before, fell back into Muslim hands in 1187.

ISLAM ASCENDANT

The significance of Baldwin IV's victory can hardly be exaggerated: it was the first real setback Saladin had suffered – and so spectacular. The exploits of Eudes de Saint-Amand and his Knights Templar seemed the more heroic for their taking place against so accomplished, so seemingly invincible, an enemy.

As the next few years went by, Baldwin's sickness strengthened its hold on him. He had to make his brother-in-law Guy de Lusignan (c. 1150–94; reigned 1186–94) his regent; and, a few years later, his successor on the throne.

His personal qualities and charisma apart, Saladin was a more formidable foe than the Crusaders had latterly been facing precisely because he had united the Muslim Middle East under his rule. Prior to this, Fatimid Egypt and Seljuk-dominated Syria had gone their own ways. Now, behind Saladin, they pulled together. Montgisard had mattered so much because it had been so obviously against the 'run' of things. It had given the Crusaders hope they hadn't hitherto dared harbour.

In 1187, Saladin made a renewed attempt to recover Jerusalem. He's said to have been personally provoked – Crusaders in a recent raid had raped his sister – though the reality is that he would have wanted to move against the Kingdom at some point, anyway. Whatever was driving him, he was inexorable, though, and this was bad news for his Christian enemies.

COURAGE IN ADVERSITY

That the brave but hopelessly outnumbered Hospitaller-led force that went out to meet Saladin at the Spring of Cresson that May Day was all but annihilated was only to be expected, perhaps; but defeat at the Battle of the Horns of Hattin (4 July) was much harder to accept. Named for the distinctly-shaped ridges that curved down from the volcanic peak in whose shade the action was fought, the engagement was to be among the most important

Above: This fifteenth-century French miniature seems accurate enough in its representation of the extent to which the Crusaders were outnumbered at the Battle of Hattin in 1187.

of the Middle Ages. Hundreds of European knights were killed in the battle itself, while Guy de Lusignan, now King of Jerusalem, was taken prisoner, and the balance of power in the Middle East dramatically upset.

The battle itself was appropriately epic in its scale. Anything up to 20,000 Crusaders – including not just knights but mounted men-at-arms and lightly equipped turcopoles as well as infantry – faced as many as 30,000 Saracens, largely cavalry. It was epic in its tone as well: the sound of the Templars' advance was 'like the loud humming of bees', recalled an awestruck Saracen who'd had to face them: they were 'horrible in arms, their whole bodies covered with triple mail'. Be that as it may, they turned out to be vulnerable: Saladin had the grass before them set alight, so their eyes would be stung to blindness and their throats and lungs thrown into spasms by the smoke; he ordered his archers to shoot the horses out from underneath them and bring them down. 'The mountains and plains, the hills and valleys all around were covered with their dead,' said another Saracen witness.

Below: This late medieval manuscript illustration shows Saracen soldiers seizing the True Cross and bearing it off in triumph following their victory at Hattin.

I saw the fallen banners sullied with dust and blood. I saw their heads broken and battered, their limbs scattered abroad, their blackened corpses piled one on top of another like the stones of a building. I remembered the words of the Koran: *'The infidel shall say, "What am I but dust?"'*

The ultimate ignominy (and a real spiritual shock: we really shouldn't underestimate this aspect) for the Crusaders was that their relic of the True Cross was captured. That, in the battle's aftermath, Saladin had scores of captured Hospitallers and Templars unceremoniously executed underlines how far they too had become talismanic in their way.

A KINGDOM COLLAPSES

The aftermath of this defeat saw the Crusader kingdom crumbling alarmingly. Guy de Lusignan's capture symbolized the overall implosion of the state. Hattin had hollowed out its defensive infrastructure: troops, flocking to reinforce the army on the battlefield, had left their castles largely ungarrisoned. In the weeks and months that followed, more than 30 fell.

LADIES TORE THEIR RICHEST ROBES AND CROPPED THEIR HAIR AS MARKS OF PENITENCE.

So too did the cities they had been protecting. By 4 September, Ascalon, so hard won, was back in Muslim hands. In Beirut, Tyre and Jerusalem, the Christian population panicked, lamenting the sinfulness they believed could be the only explanation for this abandonment by their God.

Ladies tore their richest robes and cropped their hair as marks of penitence: some stood naked in tubs of cold water on the slopes of Calvary, where Christ had died. Queen Sibylla (c. 1160–90; reigned 1186–90) led a barefoot procession of leading priests and nobles through Jerusalem to the Church of the Holy Sepulchre.

The few surviving Knights Templar in the capital took more practical steps to save the city, leading a rag-tag army, largely comprised of old men and boys. But they couldn't withstand the sheer force of the Saracens' attack, the arrows showering down like 'raindrops'. St John's Hospital was overwhelmed by the numbers of the wounded and the dying.

Opposite: Saladin looks on as a line of Christian prisoners file before him after his conquest of Jerusalem in 1187.

Saladin's threats to avenge in kind the massacres of 1099 when he took Jerusalem weren't to be realized – whether through magnanimity or strategy on his part. The defenders had threatened to destroy the city's Islamic shrines, and this may have helped encourage his willingness to spare the citizenry in return for a ransom. (Though the fact that he was subsequently prepared, in response to their pleas, to reduce this ransom perhaps suggests that he'd been intending to take the high road, for whatever reason, all along.)

Inevitably, his first action on retaking the city was stripping its Muslim monuments of their recently added Christian trappings – so the Templars' 'Temple' was once again the Al-Aqsa Mosque. There does appear to have been a certain amount of rape and pillage – later stories of Saladin's high chivalry were to some extent exaggerated – but certainly nothing like the mayhem that followed the city's capture in the First Crusade.

LATER STORIES OF SALADIN'S HIGH CHIVALRY WERE TO SOME EXTENT EXAGGERATED.

Those citizens who could afford it paid a ransom to Jerusalem's new occupiers and were allowed to leave – largely for Tyre, the Crusaders' main remaining stronghold now, along with Antioch, where the surviving Knights Templar seem to have relocated. The Hospitallers were allowed to maintain a minimal presence in Jerusalem for a year, so St John's Hospital could continue with its work. The rest of the Order had to quit the capital, left effectively homeless for the next few years. After a year's captivity in Damascus, Guy de Lusignan was set free, ready to take his place with Europe's kings in the Third Crusade.

THE THIRD CRUSADE

The Third Crusade is often referred to as the 'Crusade of Kings', because it was led by Kings Richard I, 'the Lionheart', of England (1157–99; reigned 1189–99), Philip II of France (1165–1223; reigned 1180–1223) and the Holy Roman Emperor Frederick I Barbarossa (1122–90; reigned 1155–90). In no time at all they were one king down, though. The Emperor – who set off in 1188, many months before his fellow monarchs – drowned while crossing a river in hostile territory in Anatolia en route to the Holy Land. Duke Leopold V of Austria (1157–94) tried to take up the reins, but wasn't able to in the ensuing panic and a huge German army was practically wiped out.

Leopold made it through, though with only a few thousand troops he could do little to assist the Crusader King Guy of Jerusalem, who was then bogged down in a stalemate with Saladin outside Acre. The port city was vital to the Christians,

THE TEUTONIC KNIGHTS

A CATALOGUE OF MISFORTUNES and flounces having left the Germans officially unrepresented at the Third Crusade, a group of ardent individuals took matters into their own hands. Hence the foundation of the Order of Brothers of the German House of Holy Mary in Jerusalem – or, as they have become popularly known, the Teutonic Knights.

Though the Order was formed at Acre, at the height of the seaport city's siege, its foundation could arguably be seen as having been set in motion a few years before. The loss of Jerusalem in 1187, and the consequent expulsion (and, for the moment, marginalization) of the Knights Hospitaller, had spurred merchants in Bremen and Lübeck into funding a few field hospitals. The Siege of Acre became a natural focus for this sort of work, and these hospitals in their turn became the natural focus around which a new Hospitaller-style order could emerge. Like the Hospitallers, it quickly extended its role, first of all taking on protective duties;

then going the full Templar to make itself a military order, operating out of a hilltop headquarters at Montfort (or, now, in German, Starkenberg) Castle, northeast of Nahariya, in Galilee.

Above: The Teutonic Knights wore a white surcoat with a black cross – later to be the basis of the modern military 'Iron Cross'.

who could not hope to hold on to Jerusalem (in the event of their retaking it) without some safe way of bringing in supplies. Both the Templars and Hospitallers were in the thick of the action. The Hospitallers brought up siege engines to help lead the assault on Acre.

Not until 1191 did Philip and Richard arrive and the Third Crusade get under way in earnest. As it happens, Richard's fleet was under the command of the Templars' Grand Master Robert de Sablé (1150–93; in office 1191–2). An experienced naval commander, he used his English vessels to mount a blockade on Acre from the seaward side, tightening the screws on the

Below: The execution of 2700 Saracen prisoners on the orders of England's King Richard I could not help but harden Saladin's attitude towards his foes.

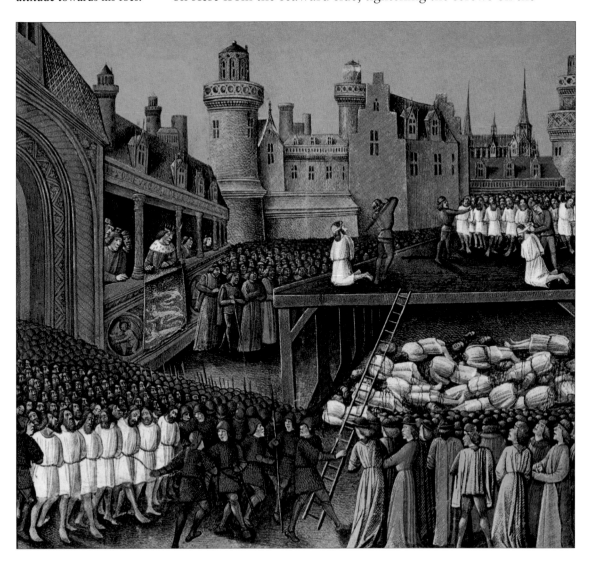

city that much further. Together with the reinforcements he and
Richard had brought with them, and Philip's Franks, the balance
of the siege was tipped and the town was taken. Meanwhile, the
Hospitallers' ships were to prove vital in the defence of Tyre when
the inevitable counter-attack came from Saladin and his forces.

Negotiations between Richard and Saladin, at first amicable,
turned nasty when – apparently believing that the Turkish leader
was tricking him – the English king had 2700 Muslim prisoners
put to death. Saladin replied with mass-executions of his
Christian captives. There was rancour within the Crusader camp
as well, despite the efforts of the Templars to broker agreement
over tactics between their commander-kings. Despite their best
efforts, a disgruntled Duke Leopold took himself off home.
Meanwhile, Philip had to leave following reports of unrest back
in France.

ARSUF AND AFTER

This left Richard alone at the head of the Third Crusade, but the
Lionheart was undaunted. Leaving Acre on 22 August 1191, he
marched his army south to where they could find themselves food
and water. The Knights Templar and Hospitaller
went in the vanguard and the rear. The going was
slow: they were harried by Saladin's mounted
archers every inch of the way, but Richard's bowmen
kept up their own hail of arrows as they went to
keep the attackers at a harmless distance.

> HE MARCHED HIS ARMY
> SOUTH TO WHERE THEY
> COULD FIND THEMSELVES
> FOOD AND WATER.

To their right, the cavalry were able to make
progress more or less safely, while beyond them the baggage
train lurched along, shielded by both the infantry and horse.
Their ships tracked them down the coast, to see off any threat
from the seaward side. Under Richard's inspirational leadership
– and calmed by the confident presence of the Templars and
Hospitallers at their front and rear – the army kept its composure
as it inched along.

The king's aims, in fact, went further than keeping his army
intact: he hoped that his apparently beleaguered situation would
tempt the enemy into a full-scale charge. On 7 September, at

Above: Richard I, 'the Lionheart', was famous for leading from the front. Here he wields his mace at the Battle of Arsuf.

Arsuf, just north of Jaffa, that moment came. The pressure from Saladin's forces became so unrelentingly intense that – in a rare breakdown in discipline – the Knights Hospitaller and Templar broke in their frustration and counter-charged. Fortunately, they carried all before them and, the momentum remaining with his force, Richard was able to regain control as general.

The final result was inconclusive. Saladin had suffered a setback, sure, and Richard's reputation had been boosted, but it was hard to see any real benefits from his victory. He himself was recalled to England soon after, having firmly cemented his place in history but having failed to win Jerusalem back from the Saracens. Talks continued, and by 1192, the right had been won for western pilgrims to visit the Holy Places in Jerusalem – but the city lay, firmly as ever, in Muslim hands.

If it hadn't quite been a failure, the Third Crusade could hardly be said to have succeeded. The military orders had to take their share in that ignominy. From their own, much narrower, more parochial perspective, though, they'd come out of the experience well and were ready to greet the new century from a position of strength. Not only had they shown great courage, resourcefulness and resilience in battle, but they had demonstrated qualities of discreet and intelligent leadership behind the scenes. Time and again, over the past few years, they'd taken up the slack when secular leaders – in Jerusalem, in the Middle East or back in Europe – had been found wanting.

A renewed programme of building bodied forth that new importance on the ground in the Holy Land. The Hospitallers built themselves a spectacular headquarter-castle on the northern edge of Acre; the Templars had their own imposing complex on the city's southwestern side. A 350m (1150ft) tunnel connected the Templar fortress with the harbour down below, so they could be readily resupplied in case of siege.

Left: A marvel of medieval engineering, the Templars' tunnel in Acre left them all but invulnerable to any siege.

Below: The Emblem of the Knights of St Thomas.

THE KNIGHTS OF ST THOMAS

ANOTHER, specifically English, military order was established in the aftermath of Acre, by one William, Chaplain to Ralph de Diceto, Dean of St Paul's in London. The Knights of St Thomas were named not for the 'doubting' apostle but for medieval England's martyr, whose reputation was continuing to inspire.

Like the Hospitallers, and the Teutonic Order, the Knights of St Thomas started out as care-givers, graduating to a wider, protective role a little later. They also pursued a fundraising role with a view to ransoming prisoners from the Saracens (though the contacts and structures they built up this way also allowed them to enrich themselves).

Not until the time of the Fifth Crusade would they be more fully militarized at the initiative of the French-born Bishop of Winchester, Peter des Roches (?–1238; in office 1205–38), an enthusiast for the crusading cause.

Comment le roy saint loys en cuidant retorner a dumete fut prins. le .vviij.e chappre. *

pres ceste desconfitu re ainsi faitte sur les sarrazins ne demoura gueires apres que

le filz du souday mort ut des puttes dorient z auua a la massore et le recoiut les egipitens a grande reue rence z honneur comme leur

4

MIGHT AND MYSTIQUE

The thirteenth century saw the military orders for the most part being bested in the field of battle. But they were nevertheless gradually growing in power and prestige.

HOLY GRAIL has come to mean a range of things to a variety of people in the modern lexicon. For a politician, perhaps a taxation system that raises money without alienating voters; for a competitive gymnast or dancer, a perfect 10 score. Figuratively, as it is used today, the 'Holy Grail' can be anything we want it to be – as long as it's the thing we would most love to have (but fear we can't).

Yet the instability we find in the phrase's modern meaning was there at the very start, in those medieval romances that couldn't make up their minds whether it was a salver or a cup. In some accounts, it was the dish from which Jesus served his apostles the paschal lamb at the Last Supper; in others it was the goblet from which he drank.

Opposite: The Crusaders came badly unstuck at the Battle of al-Mansurah in 1285.

That the chalice seems to have won out in recent popular versions of the story might merely be because it still features in the modern mass. By contrast (for a generation that doesn't often see the sacred banquet represented visually), the dish has slipped into oblivion. Yet we've no clear way of knowing that this is actually the reason. Nor, really, does it matter: the essence of the grail is its elusiveness. In Wolfram von Eschenbach's *Parzival* (the romance, which did more than any other to establish the idea of the mystic grail-quest), the grail turned out to be neither a chalice nor a dish but a precious stone.

It's been a bit like that with the Knights Templar and, to a lesser extent, the other military orders. There's a quasi-mythical character to their fame. We've already seen that they really existed, and that they had an important impact on medieval history. Even so, they seem the stuff of legend. Partly, of course, because – just like the secular knights of their time – they

Below: Wolfram von Eschenbach dictates *Parzival* (early thirteeth century), perhaps the most famous articulation of the Grail myth.

conformed to a moral and aesthetic code laid out in literary form in the romances of their time.

These stories in their turn – and in their own extravagantly stylized way – reflected contemporary realities. Looking back across so many centuries, it's all but impossible for us to distinguish clear demarcations between the different narratives of history and of fiction. Given the closeness with which medieval military, political and courtly practice modelled themselves on ideals drawn from literature and art, it can't have been that much easier even then.

HISTORIOGRAPHICAL SLIPS?

Chrétien de Troyes, as his name suggests, was either born or was otherwise associated with the very town in Aube, east-central France, in which the Order of the Knights Templar had been formally established, in January 1129. There are no coincidences, said Sigmund Freud (1856–1939), and, acting on the same assumption, populist scholars have pounced on this connection between the Grail Legend and the Knights Templar.

The poet actually *was* a Knight of the Order, we're confidently assured – though the basis for any such assertion is obscure. Granted, the Council of Troyes was a key event in the Templars' history, but Chrétien could only have been a child, if that, when it was held. Nor is there anything much in the way of evidence to point to a continuing relationship – once the Council had transacted its business, then packed up and left – between the Order of the Knights Templar and the town.

Chrétien's earliest written works date from the 1170s or after; his masterpiece, *Perceval*, from the 1180s. The Council of Troyes was ancient history by then. Besides, as important as his poem may have been in establishing the idea of the grail as a symbol, its full significance was only to be developed by other writers in subsequent decades.

Freud might have been usefully employed analysing the unconscious compulsions compelling such a confident bundling together of history, myth and metaphor. Like the other Arthurian

THEY CONFORMED TO A MORAL AND AESTHETIC CODE LAID OUT IN THE ROMANCES OF THEIR TIME.

Above: Pope Honorius II gives the Knights Templar his official blessing. Relations with the hierarchy weren't always to run so smoothly.

romances, *Perceval* can be seen to draw on deeper symbolisms, Christian and pagan, and on even older, more elemental anxieties and fears. But what goes for internet pseudo-historians holds too for the chroniclers of much earlier times – and understandably: myth-making was a considerable part of what the military orders were about. That and simply getting by, of course.

SUPPORTING THE WAR EFFORT
Much of the military orders' most important work was done day in, day out, many hundreds of miles from the fronts of war and – quite frankly – could hardly have been much more mundane. It cost money to kit out a knight-at-arms (horses, weaponry and armour, clothes, food and drink and lodging at home and on the road), and a great deal of money to keep a company of them supplied. The Knights Templar and Hospitaller met these costs the same way their secular equivalents did with the profits from their lands.

Opposite: Its barns and gardens restored in modern times, Cressing Temple, Essex, was one of many Templar 'preceptories'.

The Knights Templar alone had in the region of a thousand 'preceptories' – monastic estates – scattered from Spain to

Scotland and from France to Croatia. Approximately 140 similar estates in the Holy Land itself gave more immediate support to Templar communities on the ground. Generally these lands had been given as donations by pious and public-spirited individuals who hoped to do themselves some good in the next life by doing good in this one. Conventionally, under the feudal system, serfs were attached to the land they worked, so these estates came to the Order as fully functioning economic units.

At Cressing Temple in Essex, England, for example, a manor was granted to the Templars in 1136 by Matilda of Boulogne (c. 1105–52), Queen Consort to King Stephen (c. 1092–1154; reigned 1135–54). Its 5600 ha (14,000 acres) were distributed across 160 smaller tenant farms: along with residential buildings, a chapel, stables, dairies, a dovecot, granaries and barns, there were wind- and watermills, a bakery, a brewery and a blacksmith's forge. Altogether, then, a big and productive profit centre from which the proceeds were directed to the war effort of the Order as a whole.

Cressing Temple stood out in its sheer scale: much of the Templars' land came to them in considerably smaller blocs. Like the 180 ha (450 acres) they had in the South Downs at Saddlescombe Farm, for instance.

Penhill was only one of ten such holdings the Order had in Yorkshire. It all added up, though, and the Templars' lands were vast and on the whole extremely well-managed – the Knights were very organized and utterly clear in their aims.

PRECEPTORIES AND PLACE NAMES

The Knights had several preceptories (or smaller so-called commandries) in Scotland too, many of them around the northeastern town of Nairn. But their headquarters in the country seems to have been in Midlothian, south of Edinburgh, in the village now accordingly known as 'Temple'. (Its earlier name, Balantrodoch, means 'Town of the Warriors' in Gaelic, itself apparently a reference to the Knights Templar.)

A TALE OF TWO TEMPLES

THE CENTRE OF TEMPLAR life in England was, not surprisingly, in London. The Order maintained a major preceptory in the city, where modern-day Chancery Lane meets Holborn, but this 'Old Temple' was fairly rapidly outgrown. By 1166, a more extensive 'New Temple' was being built in the area between the River Thames and Fleet Street, just above the Victoria (and Victorian) Embankment, around a handsome and prestigious Temple Church. This was completed in the 1180s.

The Knights had their own on-site orchards, market gardens, stabling for horses, and accommodation for other livestock. A considerable staff would have been needed to keep these going – even without the number of servants, cooks, stewards and officials of various sorts who would have been needed to look after the Grand Master and his knights. They also had industrial facilities, from blacksmiths' forges to water mills. If they were consequently important employers, the Knights became significant landlords in the area as well, letting out houses up and down Fleet Street and into nearby Charing. (Now famous for its 'Charing Cross', placed there in the 1390s, this little slice of central London was at this time a quiet village.)

Of even this newer centre, however, little of the physical fabric now remains. Again, the most enduring feature has been the 'Temple' name. As two of the historic 'Inns of Court', however, offering lodgings, office space and institutional representation to London's lawyers over several centuries, the 'Inner Temple' and 'Middle Temple' have a quasi-monastic flavour in both architecture and atmosphere. (The Middle Temple's cloisters weren't built till many centuries later, but seem to occupy the exact same site as the Templars' had.)

It's as a place-name element that the Order's memory chiefly survives in the British Isles: Templetown, County Wexford, in Ireland; Temple Sowerby, Cumbria; Temple Dinsley, Hertfordshire; Temple Ewell, Kent; Temple Bruer, Lincolnshire; Temple Guiting, Gloucestershire; the little hamlet of Temple, on Cornwall's Bodmin Moor…

Sometimes, there are intriguing traces of a Templar life at one time lived here, as at Templecombe, Somerset, with its celebrated 'Christ'. Now much-faded, this panel-painting of a bearded (but, significantly, un-haloed) head may not show Christ at all: could this be John the Baptist rather than the Saviour? Or rather, could it be the mysterious (and maybe more sinister) bearded head that was said to be held up at Templar ceremonies for veneration – for idolatrous adoration even, it was charged.

All these examples, and many more, point to the extensiveness of the Templar presence, the extent to which they were embedded in these countries' civil life. Here, on the 'home front', as far as can be imagined from the blood and thunder of war, more everyday, humdrum heroics went on.

The same pattern was replicated across much of Western Europe. At Coulommiers, northeast of Paris in the Île de France;

Below: Modern, as well as medieval, writers have been drawn to the stories of the Templars. Rosslyn Chapel, Midlothian, Scotland, was made famous by Dan Brown.

at Sergeac, in the Dordogne; at Tomar, the Templars' main centre in Portugal, in the Ribatejo region; and at San Servando, outside Toledo, Spain. (The Templars' Iberian holdings of course continued to see military action long after those in France and England did. They were generally centred on strongly-fortified working castles.)

Agriculture may have been the main economic focus for the Order – as it was for Western Europe at this time – but other areas were explored as well. At Lissewege, north of Bruges, in Belgium, a thriving textile centre grew up under the supervision of the Knights Templar.

HOSPITAL HOLDINGS

Not to be outdone, the Knights Hospitaller had preceptories of their own, across much of Western Europe. Again, the majority were working farms, like the ones at Halston, outside Whittington in Shropshire, or Swingfield, northwest of Folkestone, Kent, but they also owned and operated manufactures and mills. Some of these were of considerable size, like the 'tide mill' on the Thames at Horsleydown, Bermondsey, London.

Below: Spain's San Servando Castle was already a Benedictine monastery when the Knights Templar fortified it in the twelfth century.

A similar mill on the Liffey at Kilmainham, Dublin, was built on such a scale that it prevented the proper navigation of shipping, and caused a serious dispute with the city's merchants in 1220. Despite being asked to by no less a personage than King Henry III, the Hospitallers refused to back down, and their mill remained.

The Hospitallers also had forestry interests in Aragon, Spain; they mined for lead, gold and silver in Sicily, and in 1373 were recorded as having their own colliery in Fenham, Newcastle-upon-Tyne.

MOVING MONEY

Alongside the profits from such enterprises, the military orders continued to receive gifts more directly (whether as simple donations or as property surrendered by their own applicants on enlisting). They accordingly became fantastically rich. As religious orders, however, they were fantastically well-respected too: no one would have dreamt of doubting their probity or good faith. Given their substantial contribution to the economic life of Western Europe and their military presence on the ground in the Middle East, moreover, their influence seemed to span the crusading world.

Above: This castle at Consuegra, near Toledo, Spain, was given to the Knights Hospitaller by King Alfonso VIII (1155–1214; reigned 1158–1214).

That the crusading ideal exacted major costs in courage and commitment is obvious. The risk of falling in the field of battle was very real. So too were the dangers of succumbing to disease, of dying of thirst and starvation in the mountains of Anatolia or the deserts of Palestine; or of being shipwrecked on the voyage out or home. But the financial costs were great as well – and not just the outlays required for arms and equipment, travel and sustenance abroad. What, meanwhile, was to become of property and savings at home – effectively abandoned while the knight went off to the Holy Land, not to return for many months or even years?

It seems to have been informally, and by very slow degrees, that the Knights Templar took up the role of bankers. Secular knights naturally turned to them for support with the financial problems that they faced. A credit note issued by a Templar scribe in England could assure his fellow monk in Palestine that its bearer was 'good' for a grant, which could then be repaid afterwards when he got home. Likewise, a letter from Jerusalem or Acre could prompt a deduction from moneys held in trust by Templars in the Loire or Leicestershire. The rudimentary basis of a banking system was in place.

A CRIMINAL CRUSADE

Holy War was what it was all about, though, and, as the thirteenth century started, the military orders were a very real and powerful presence on the ground in the Middle East. They might easily have had a powerful presence in the action of the Fourth Crusade (1202–4), had that venture actually made it to its intended theatre of war. As it turned out, it was a good bit of history to miss.

The rulers of Venice and Genoa, who were providing sea transport and were keen to make a killing on the contract, ended up in wrangling, rancorous dispute with the Crusaders. With

Below: Eugène Delacroix's view of the entry of the Crusaders into Constantinople (1202): a shameful spree of violence was to ensue.

no agreement in sight, the Venetian Doge Enrico Dandolo (c. 1107–1205; in office 1192–1205) decided to take advantage of having so many men under arms aboard the vessels of his city's fleet by attacking the Adriatic port of Zara, which had been resisting Venetian domination. Some Crusaders heeded the Pope's insistent warnings and refused to attack another Catholic city. Even so, Zara was besieged and sacked.

BANKING BACKLASH

'No one,' we've said, would have dreamt of doubting the Knights Templar order's 'probity or good faith'. Unfortunately, if this was the case to start with, it wouldn't last too long. That kind of confidence is a wasting asset – it is, at least, in the popular imagination. Although men of the world, of wealth and rank, and institutions of influence would continue to rely on the Templars' integrity, their image among the populace at large was to be slowly – and at first imperceptibly – compromised.

Modern capitalism – modern life, indeed – wouldn't have been possible without the banking industry and its ability to collect, marshal and distribute money in vast sums where it's most needed. Not in the social justice sense of the terms 'distribute' and 'need', of course – bankers have been understandably berated for their indifference to those things – but in the economic development sense for sure. We couldn't have had the last few hundred years, with their industrial or IT revolutions, without the facilities banks' provided in start-up funding – and ongoing support – for ambitious economic ventures of every kind.

But the banker's role is by definition discreet – which means that it comes across to the public as impersonal or

Above: Fund-raising for the Crusades was taken as seriously as any military campaign. Here, monks collect contributions for the cause.

faceless. Bankers, it is feared, are society's 'secret masters', pulling strings behind the scenes. That fear is of course kin to the centuries-old paranoia about the Jews – also damned by their association with the financial-services industry. Demagogues and conspiracists were keen to talk up the 'threat' they posed. Banking may have made the Templars (even more) rich; it may have helped them perform invaluable services to society; but it also made them the object of profound suspicion.

The quarrel over payment remaining unresolved, the Venetians diverted to Constantinople and landed their passengers there – all armed and kitted up, with nowhere to go. One 'other' being much like another, they set about sacking Constantinople and slaughtering its people; raping, burning and looting for a full three days.

Below: Christian knights prove their piety by slaughtering Cathars in the Albigensian Crusade.

CLEAN HANDS AGAINST THE CATHARS

THE MIDDLE AGES MAY have been an 'Age of Faith' – but the more strongly religious ideals were held, the greater the risk of disillusion when reality fell short. By the twelfth century, the wealth and power of the Church, and its cosy association with those who oppressed the people, were giving rise to widespread discontent.

Some rejected Christianity altogether, like the Cathars (in Greek the 'Pure People')

of the Languedoc, southern France. Theirs was a dualistic universe in which God and Satan warred and body and soul were locked in eternal opposition. The soul was eternal and belonged in heaven, the realm of God, of light. All that was material and mortal belonged to this world – that of Satan – and was dark and bad. Since Christ was 'the Word made flesh', he and his teachings must be evil too. The worldliness

DOWN IN THE DELTA

The only serious atrocities involved in the Fifth Crusade (1217–21) were organizational. As far as it went, the part played by the Knights Templar and other orders was exemplary. The idea behind this crusade had been a novel one: to attack Jerusalem indirectly, via Egypt, to which end the Christian forces

Below: The seal of Raymond VI, who distinguished himself by his support for the Cathars.

of the Church was only too clear: far from being the 'Bride of Christ', preached Cathar Arnald Hot, it was 'espoused of the Devil and its doctrine diabolical'.

Such teachings tapped into a deep well of frustrated idealism, and found many followers. As far as Pope Innocent III (c. 1160–1216; reigned 1198–1216) was concerned, Catharism could not be ignored. The heretics were like the Saracens, he said, in 1209, proclaiming a crusade against this enemy within.

The 'Albigensian Crusade' was hideously one-sided: it took its name from the town of Albi, a hotbed of the heresy. For months and then for years on end, this cruel 'crusade' continued, large and fully equipped armies – including mounted knights, foot soldiers, archers and crossbowmen – deployed against unarmed civilians. Sappers with siege engines smashed their way through the walls of provincial cities.

At Béziers, 20,000 men, women and children were put to the sword, the Papal Legate boasted. Over a thousand were burned alive in the supposed 'sanctuary' of a church. Though, from about 1213, the Pope tried to rein in the carnage, it had acquired an unstoppable momentum. Ultimately as many as a million may have died.

The Knights Templar and Hospitaller seem to have steered clear of this monstrous persecution. Why mention it then? Could their very avoidance of the conflict have been significant – a 'dog that didn't bark'? Many modern researchers have been intrigued by what might otherwise seem a surprising 'virtue of omission' and wondered whether it might not point to a more serious engagement in Cathar theology on the orders' part.

Count Raymond VI of Toulouse (1156–1222), who stood out among France's nobility in his sympathy and support for the suffering Cathars, came from a long crusading line, of course. His family had established a connection with the military orders over generations. We've no real reason to think that he – or, in their turn, the military orders – had any more mystic motives in refusing to join in the holocaust.

were landed at Damietta, on the eastern edge of the Nile Delta. King Andrew II of Hungary (c. 1177–1235) led the main attack, with a clutch of German princes. Emperor Frederick II (1194–1250; reigned 1220–5) was expected to join the Crusade, but had not yet arrived.

Guillaume of Chartres (c. 1178–1218; in office 1210–18) led the Knights Templar, though he was taken sick and died after being wounded in the Siege of Damietta. The Hospitallers took the lead in this operation, lining up their ships in the Nile beneath the city walls as floating platforms for siege ladders, under cover of catapult and trebuchet bombardment from the far bank.

The siege was tough, but successfully concluded; the defeated Sultan even came to terms. Saladin's younger brother, Al-Adil I (1145–1218; reigned 1200–18), or 'Saphadin', had been badly weakened by the succession struggle he had not long won. Caught off-guard by this fresh invasion, and focused on possessions

Below: The Siege of Damietta (1217–18) brought the Crusaders a rare victory, though casualties among the town's inhabitants were very high.

further to the east in southern Anatolia and Iraq, he was happy enough to cut a deal. He was, he assured the Crusaders, content to let them have the Kingdom of Jerusalem, with the exception of a couple of key castles in northeastern Syria.

IMPREGNABLE

Above: Still imposing, even in its ruined state, the Château de Pèlerin dominates the coast at Atlit, Israel.

ONE MORE SUBSTANTIAL PRODUCT of the Fifth Crusade was the impressive fortress at Atlit, south of Haifa, on Israel's northern coast – traditionally known as Château Pèlerin, or 'Pilgrim's Castle'. It was built by the Knights Templar, who started work on its construction early in 1218. Strategically sited on a rocky headland, it replaced a nearby, much smaller Crusaders' castle (Le Destroit), which was now 'slighted' – deliberately demolished – so the Saracens couldn't use it.

Pilgrim's Castle was massive. It could accommodate a garrison of some 4000. It was formidably solid, its outer 'curtain' wall over 15m (50ft) high and 6m (20ft) thick. Three projecting towers gave defenders a clear shot across the outside face of the wall to discourage attempts to storm or undermine it. Beyond that, the inner wall rose an intimidating 30m (98ft), protected in its turn by its own three towers. A concealed harbour allowed the stronghold to be resupplied by sea. Essentially, as the Sultan Al-Mu'azzam Isa (1176–1227; reigned 1218–27) was to find in 1220, it could comfortably hold out against a siege forever.

But the Pope's officials, confident that, once the emperor appeared, they'd be able to have the entire kingdom without any concessions at all, refused to let the leaders on the ground agree to this. The months went by, supplies grew short and, slowly, imperceptibly but inexorably the victorious Crusaders found their position weakening. Eventually, they were cowering in the Delta, thoroughly bogged down and beaten. Of Emperor Frederick II there was still no sign.

Instead, reinforcements arrived from the east, in support of Saphadin: the Crusaders suddenly found themselves surrounded. In the words of Guillaume de Chartres' friend and successor, Peire de Montagut (?–1232; in office 1218–32), an Aragonese Reconquista veteran, 'We were without food … caught like fish in a net.' Victory had somehow slowly slipped away into humiliating defeat. They hadn't even actually made it to the Holy Land.

FADING FORTUNES

Frederick II did go some way towards redeeming himself when, in the Sixth Crusade of 1228, he negotiated the return of Jerusalem diplomatically from the Sultan al-Kamil (c. 1177–1238; reigned 1218–38). Among the concessions he had to make was, revealingly, the promise not to help fund the Knights Templar or Hospitaller, a measure of the seriousness with which the Sultan took them. Jerusalem was in any case recaptured in July 1244, when a newly-arriving tribe of Turks, the Khwarezmiyya, invaded the Holy Land and took Jerusalem. The Christian population of the city was either expelled or massacred. An attempt to turn the Khwarezmiyya back in a pitched battle at La Forbie (now Harbiyah, northeast of Gaza) that October proved over-

Below: Frederick II's siege engines didn't succeed in taking Jerusalem but they put its defenders under so much pressure that they came to terms.

ambitious – especially when the Egyptian Sultan sent an army of his Mamluks (Turkic slave-soldiers) in support.

The engagement ended in a bloodbath. The Knights Hospitaller lost their master, Walter of Brienne (1205–44), along with scores of men; the Templars over 280 of the 300 of their knights who'd joined the fray. As for the crusading movement as a whole, that lost its last best chance of recovering Jerusalem, which was to remain in Muslim hands until the twentieth century.

THE END OF AN IDEAL

The final significant flowering of the crusading idea came with the Seventh Crusade (1248–54), which was led by France's King Louis IX (St Louis, 1214–70; reigned 1226–70). Again, the idea was to attack from the west, through Egypt. Louis took with him an army of 15,000, including his mounted knights, his regular infantry and crossbowmen. After a promising start, Louis' army was heavily defeated by an army of Mamluks led by Baibars (c. 1223–77). Al Malik as-Salih (1205–49; reigned 1240–9) was killed by the Templars

on the battlefield – though only two out of 282 Knights Templar were to survive what turned into a rout for the crusading side.

To add insult to injury, the French king himself was captured with his knights and held to ransom. Not only that, but within a matter of months as-Salih's son and short-lived successor Al-Muazzam Turanshah (?–1250; reigned 1249–50) was assassinated in the course of a Mamluk coup. The slaves were now the masters in the Middle East.

Above: Louis IX sets out with his fleet from France – bound for the Holy Land at the start of the Seventh Crusade.

As for European power in the region, that was nowhere to be seen. The Mamluks extended their influence eastward from Egypt into Syria, taking the Templar strongholds at Safed (1266) and Beaufort Castle (1268). In 1270, apparently unfazed, Louis IX embarked on an Eighth Crusade, but he made it only as far as Tunis, where he died. A Ninth Crusade led by Prince Edward 'Longshanks' – later to be King Edward I (1239–1307; reigned 1272–1307) of England – began the following year, but the future 'Hammer of the Scots' was to fare less well against the Mamluks.

Right: Louis IX was going to need every bit of saintly patience he could muster after he was captured at al-Mansurah (1250).

They added Chastel Blanc ('White Castle', taken from the Templars) and the Hospitallers' prestigious Crac des Chevaliers to their portfolio of fortresses at this time.

'ANCIENT TREACHERY'

CONSPIRACY THEORIES HAVE OF course dogged the military orders down into the present day. We shouldn't be too scathing: if they've created the need for a more sober historiography, they've created the interest as well. It's as important as it's intriguing to know, however, that this kind of paranoia was present even comparatively early in the orders' history.

Robert I, the Count of Artois (1216–50) fell at Al-Mansurah, Egypt, in the course of the Seventh Crusade. He'd ordered an unauthorized and hot-headed assault on the fort there with his men. Before the attack, the leader of the troop of Knights Templar who were with him made clear his strong (and evidently justified) disapproval. The Count, contemporary chroniclers reported, denounced the Templars – and the military orders more generally – in terms which were to become only too recognizable in the centuries that followed:

Oh ancient treachery of the Temple! Oh, old sedition of the Hospitallers! Oh fraud long-concealed, now you burst out openly into our midst. This is what we have predicted and foreseen for a long time, and it was truly predicted, that this whole eastern land would have been captured long ago if our forces had not been impeded by the fraud of the Temple and the Hospital and of others who claim to be religious ... For the Templars fear and the Hospitallers and their accomplices are afraid that if the land is subdued to the Christian faith their dominion, which they feed with ample revenues, will expire.

Robert's desire to have a scapegoat for anticipated failure may be all too clear, but the specifics of his condemnation are nevertheless interesting. The Order of the Templar had only existed for 130 years or so. Just how 'ancient' could its treachery really be?

Common to all such conspiracy theories is the way they float free of any real factual basis, behind the sketchiest show of plausibility. That they accrued around the Templars and Hospitallers was natural enough, given the aura of secrecy surrounding these orders and the incomprehension this inevitably created among outsiders. That incomprehension could only grow as the centuries went by and the medieval world and its military orders became ever more remote: that quasi-mythic status came close to displacing any historical recognition there might be.

THE AGONY OF ACRE

Twenty years later, in 1291, the Mamluks laid siege to Acre. For a month, it held out: in ferocious fighting, the Teutonic Knights in the city were wiped out completely; the Templars lost scores of men – including Grand Master Guillaume de Beaujeu (?–1291; in office 1273–91). Jean de Villiers (?–1293; in office 1285–93), the Hospitallers' Master, fought on till before, left badly wounded, he was spirited safely away to Cyprus after Acre's fall.

'There were so many Saracens', he told a friend in a letter home to France, 'that we could not count them.'

Right: The Knights Templar led the last-ditch defence of Acre in 1291. The nineteenth-century painter Domingue Papety captures the heroic scene.

*Even so, we drove them back three times ...
And in that action, and in the others in which
the brothers of our order fought for the city, for
their country and their lives, we lost – little by
little – our whole community. ...*

*I myself, that same day, was stricken almost
to death with a lance between the shoulders, a
wound which has made writing this letter most
difficult. Meanwhile, a great crowd of Saracens
was entering the city on all sides, by land and
sea, making their way along the pierced and
broken walls till they found where we were
sheltered. Our sergeants, boys and mercenaries
and crusaders gave up all hope and, throwing
down their weapons and casting off their
armour, fled for the ships.*

*We and our brothers – most of us wounded
either to death or very gravely – still fought on
as best we could, God knows. And, as some of us lay there, all
but dead, completely collapsed before our enemies, our sergeants
and our serving-boys came and carried us away, apparently
mortally wounded, at the utmost danger to themselves ...*

Above: Jean de Villiers,
Master of the Knights
Hospitaller at Acre, was
lucky to be rescued from
the field alive.

As for Acre, the attackers had no use for the place. They
calmly razed it to the ground – an emphatic conclusion to the
great age of the Crusades. A forlorn little garrison was retained
on Ruad (or Arwad), a waterless rock off the coast of Syria, some
way north of the city. But mainland Outremer was completely
Crusader-free.

TEUTONIC TROUBLES

Meanwhile, on Europe's eastern frontiers, the Baltic Slavs had
for some time been seriously restive under the shaky rule of the
Polish kings. After repeated invasions they remained obdurately
unpacified – and pagan. Again, the call went up for a 'crusade'.
It found a response in the Teutonic Knights.

From about 1230 they made a series of sweeps through
Prussia and beyond into what are now Livonia and Lithuania,

fighting – like the 'knights' they were – as armoured cavalry, followed into the field by bodies of light cavalry and infantry. In his 'Golden Bull of Rieti' (1234), Pope Gregory IX (c. 1145–1241; reigned 1227–41) had granted Prussia to the order as a 'monastic state' – in theory, at least, they were the country's rulers.

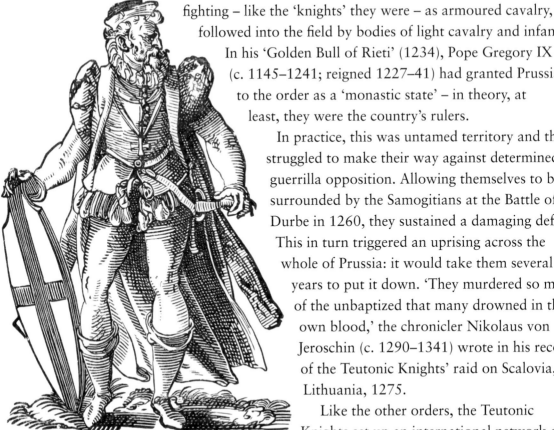

Above: Teutonic knight. After a woodcut by Jost Amman, published 1585.

In practice, this was untamed territory and they struggled to make their way against determined guerrilla opposition. Allowing themselves to be surrounded by the Samogitians at the Battle of Durbe in 1260, they sustained a damaging defeat. This in turn triggered an uprising across the whole of Prussia: it would take them several years to put it down. 'They murdered so many of the unbaptized that many drowned in their own blood,' the chronicler Nikolaus von Jeroschin (c. 1290–1341) wrote in his record of the Teutonic Knights' raid on Scalovia, Lithuania, 1275.

Like the other orders, the Teutonic Knights set up an international network of monastically administered estates – some as far-flung as Sicily and southern Greece, and in an Armenia under threat from the expanding Mamluk empire. Most of their foundations were in Prussia, and up around the Baltic coast, however – those areas they were conquering in line with the Golden Bull of Rieti.

These developments were qualitatively different from the preceptories of the Knights Templar and Hospitaller, then. They weren't just money-making operations but part of a conscious and sustained attempt to colonize, Christianize and so 'civilize' what was taken to be a wild country.

LOST ... AND FOUND

What next for the military orders? As the thirteenth century approached its end, they'd been defeated on the ground on every front. Yet their reputation was high, their mystique and their glamour only growing. Despite the setbacks they had suffered, they'd clearly conducted themselves honourably and bravely in defence of their faith – and of Christendom.

They could hardly be blamed for a geopolitical catastrophe in which the West as a whole was implicated. The continuing tendency of the medieval mind – even at this comparatively late stage – to apprehend defeat as divine chastisement for sin made contemporary critics slower than they might have been to find fault with the military orders specifically. (Though, of course, as we've already seen, there had always been those ready to dissent from the wider praise.)

All in all, their status was secure – if not in quite the political and strategic sense they might have hoped it to be. Their power was, in the modern jargon, 'soft'. But it was nevertheless impressively strong and far-reaching. If they'd lost the Holy Land, they'd gained an unbreakable hold on the imagination of the West. In this respect they had, perhaps, secured their Holy Grail.

Below: The Battle of the Ice, Lake Peipus, Russia, 1242; an illumination from a sixteenth-century chronicle.

ICED UP

THE TEUTONIC KNIGHTS DIDN'T just campaign against Prussian pagans in Eastern Europe but against the Orthodox Christians of Russia. Attacking the northern city of Novgorod in 1240, they were badly defeated two years later by Prince Alexander Nevsky (1221–63) at the famous Battle of the Ice.

Rashly, the Knights allowed themselves to be drawn out on to the frozen surface of Lake Peipus by Alexander's tactical retreat. The slipping, slithering charges of the heavily armoured Knights were repelled by a resolute Russian infantry, and they became a sitting target for Alexander's archers.

5

BEFORE A FALL

The fourteenth century found the military orders caught precariously between power and redundancy. What, with the Holy Land now lost, would be their role?

THE RECOVERY of the Holy Land had been the military orders' *raison d'être*. The fall of Acre had left them essentially adrift. One obvious way of dealing with this new situation was deep denial – carrying on as though everything was just as it had always been. The Knights Templar appear to have opted for this approach. They were as committed as ever to the recapture of Jerusalem and the Holy Places, their Grand Master Jacques de Molay (c. 1243–1314; in office 1298–1312) insisted. That remained their all-consuming mission and their goal.

Since the siege, they'd taken refuge offshore in Cyprus. They quickly came to dominate the island's politics – to the growing resentment of its king, it must be said. Though it must be added as well that, in such unhappy times, a certain degree of

Opposite: The Templars' downfall came to exemplify the fickleness of fortune for the powerful. An illustration from Giovanni Boccaccio's *On the Fall of Princes*, 1467.

Above: Cyprus became the centre for the military orders' activities. The Hospitallers and Templars had next-door churches here in Famagusta.

irascibility was to be expected. Henry II (1270–1324; reigned 1285–1324) was also – at least nominally – King of Jerusalem. He too had been dislodged from his mainland realm. (He'd never actually enjoyed authority over the city of Jerusalem itself.) It's hardly surprising that, in the confined space of Cyprus, King and Knights Templar should have trodden on each other's toes; and that in the gloomy circumstances of the post-Acre era they should have got on one another's nerves.

RATS IN A SACK

Obdurately undaunted, though, in 1302 the Templars attempted an invasion of Outremer via the island of Ruad. Henry had kept troops here against the day when some such reconquest might seem realistic. That day hadn't come, in truth, but the Templars couldn't – or at least wouldn't – wait. Inevitably, they were soon sent packing. They lost 120 knights – and King Henry his remaining Syrian stronghold – in what had been a conspicuously hopeless and pointless action.

Cyprus felt still more claustrophobic as the relationship between Henry and the Templars worsened. In 1306, they supported a coup by the king's brother, Amalric of Tyre (c. 1272–1310; reigned 1306–10) – a short-term triumph, given that he was to be assassinated, and Henry restored, just a few years later.

CHICKENS COMING HOME ...

In the longer term, the Templars had stored up difficulties for themselves. Their bullying of Henry had been brazen, their political meddling completely shameless. Cyprus might be a backwater, but the crowned heads of Europe had all been looking on, and they'd been profoundly unsettled by what they'd seen. For a century or so, they'd supported the Knights Templar as champions of Christianity in the Middle East. And fair enough: the West had shared a common purpose.

IN THE LONGER TERM, THE TEMPLARS HAD STORED UP DIFFICULTIES FOR THEMSELVES.

Why, though, would they continue to support so rich and powerful an order when there was so little certainty as to its motives or its values? Their guiding purpose gone, the Knights were going to pursue whatever policy seemed to suit them best in any given moment. Their supreme goal was their order's perpetuation and, to that end, the promotion of its immediate interests. What reason did any king or queen (or for that matter any churchman) have to place their trust in them? How was their loyalty to be relied on now?

And it only mattered the more because the Templars had dug themselves so deeply into the European establishment. Their military contributions apart, they'd won wide trust as counsellors, diplomats and power brokers. Their banking operations had brought them important economic leverage over Christian Europe's states. The political credit all these things had brought, for so many years a source of strength, now seemed a weakness, as suspicion spiralled. The bigger they'd been, the harder they were going to fall.

Opposite: Fulk de Villaret rebuilt the Order of the Knights Hospitaller as a naval force.

ALL RHODES ...

While the Knights Templar were toppling King Henry II in Cyprus, the Knights Hospitaller had been more usefully employed across the sea. And, at sea: it was clear now that what had been essentially an army of land-based knights was going to have to reinvent itself as a naval force. Under the leadership of Fulk de Villaret (?–1327; in office 1305–27), that was what it did.

The shift required an adjustment of strategy as well as of tactical training. While still insisting on its ultimate aim of reconquering the Holy Land, the Order was committed to seeking a more sensible staging post. Here, De Villaret believed, it could regroup and rebuild its forces; and from here more aggressive actions might be launched.

It found its headquarters on the island of Rhodes – nominally a Byzantine possession, but in practice dominated by the Turks. Despite which – a dog in the manger, in the Hospitallers' view – Emperor Andronicus II (1259–1332; reigned 1282–1328) refused to yield. In 1306, then, the Knights laid siege to the city of Rhodes itself.

Below: The Grand Master's Palace in Rhodes proclaimed the power of the Knights Hospitaller.

They were to be stuck there, camped out around the city but unable quite to take it, for the next three years. The Hospitallers couldn't muster sufficient strength to bring things to a quick conclusion. Neither, though, could the Byzantines, who sent three successive relief-expeditions without being able to lift the siege. Finally, in 1309, however, it fell, and the Knights Hospitaller had secured themselves a strategic base of operations. Just off the Anatolian coast, it commanded the shipping lanes of the Aegean and the eastern Mediterranean, and was the merest stone's throw from the Holy Land.

For the moment, despite the best intentions, any fresh crusade still seemed a distant prospect. Only with the utmost difficulty had Rhodes itself been taken, after

Below: Outside an intimidating castle; inside an imposing but peaceful monastery, the Grand Master's Palace reflected the Knights Hospitaller's twofold purpose.

all. The Hospitallers did, however, now have a strong and readily defensible headquarters where they could consolidate their forces. In the course of the next few years, the Order established itself in strength on the nearby islands of Cos, Kastellorizo, Symi, Tilos and Chalki.

Their security assured, they were able to rebuild their fleet. Over the next few years, they started harassing Mamluk shipping – essentially setting themselves up as pious pirates. The good fight could be fought very profitably, they realized.

A COLOSSAL COMPLEX

THE MASSIVE BRAZEN STATUE of a man, his legs bestriding the harbour entrance, the Colossus of Rhodes was one of the reputed wonders of the ancient world. If it ever existed, however, this spectacular monument has been lost a great many centuries since, so now the island must make do with one of the architectural wonders of the medieval world.

It's by no means a bad exchange, in fact: the Knights Hospitaller's castle, and Grand Master's Palace, represents all that was great and ambitious about the Order, and its age. Whilst there'd been a Byzantine fortress here since the seventh century (and there are mosaics here suggesting even earlier occupation), the Knights Hospitaller had rebuilt the place completely.

Today, this stunning citadel is a major tourist attraction, but it really isn't hard to imagine it in more warlike days gone by. At the same time, though, it seems to sum up the paradox of the Hospitaller ethos – and that of the military orders more generally: outside, with its massive towers and its crenellated walls, it's enormously intimidating; inside, it's all quiet courtyards and arcaded halls.

The Knights Templar, by cruel contrast, were finding out the hard way the high price that might have to be paid for playing high politics. As long as there had been real crusades to be fought, the Order's function had been clear. Now its power, vast but vague and ominously free-floating, unaccountable, seemed an ever-present danger to the European peace.

In part this was a real problem: the Devil does find work for idle hands. The Templars' shenanigans in Cyprus had shown this clearly. It was as much a problem of perception, though – much more so, indeed, when perceptions were carefully managed by opportunistic monarchs like Philip the Fair of France.

PAPAL POLITICS

In justice to the Knights Templar, they weren't the only ones in the Church who'd incautiously involved themselves in the secular politics of Europe's courts. The Papacy itself was in over its head. Pope Nicholas IV (1227–92; reigned 1288–92) had played with fire when he'd bought the support of Italy's powerful Colonna family with favours and agreed to crown the French prince Charles II of Anjou (1254–1309; reigned 1285–1309) King of Sicily. (It was a small world at the top in Europe at that time: Cardinal Egidio Colonna (c. 1243–1316) had, among other more public religious duties, been the boyhood tutor to Philip the Fair and his family's alliance with the French monarchy was to endure.)

The Colonna clan were in no mood to surrender their special status under Nicholas' successor, Celestine V (1215–96; reigned 1294). In his eagerness to impress his loyalty on Charles, he had gone so far as to transplant his papal court to his capital at Naples. Obviously, ignominiously, out of his depth, Celestine had abdicated, just five months after his election in 1294, making way for the much more formidable Boniface VIII (c. 1230–1303; reigned 1294–1303).

Boniface, who had restored the papacy to Rome, wasn't cowed by Charles, or by the French ascendancy he represented.

Above: Pope Nicholas IV attempted to play politics, but succeeded only in storing up trouble for the Church.

He was very quick to clash with Philip the Fair. But his confrontational manner only precipitated the coming crisis. From the first, he had both the King of Sicily and the Colonna family against him. Years of harassment led to an assassination attempt in 1303: Boniface survived but died a few weeks later.

Above: Pope Boniface rejects the Colonna family's advances.

Below: Clement V establishes his papacy in Avignon.

AUTHORITY ABDUCTED

Boniface's successor, Benedict XI (1240–1304; reigned 1303–4), was pulled this way and that by Charles and the Colonnas. The French won out after Benedict's death with the election of Clement V (c. 1264–1314; reigned 1305–14), who as Bertrand de Got had been the Archbishop of Bordeaux. He never so much as visited Rome and, four years into his reign, in 1309, formally transferred the seat of papal power to Avignon. It was to remain there, under French domination, for well over 60 years.

Even in these more sceptical, secularist times, it seems shocking that the Holy See, the centre of that power bequeathed to St Peter by Christ himself, should simply have been moved to suit the convenience of the King of France. But this was only the most obvious of Clement's concessions to Philip the Fair. No fewer than nineteen new French cardinals were created, to promote his interests in the *Curia*.

PHILIP THE UNFAIR

KING PHILIP IV (1268–1314; reigned
1285–1314) was popularly known as
Philip the Fair. Handsome is as handsome
does, they say, and Philip's fairness ended
at his face. He might as easily have gone
down in history as Philip the Feckless,
given his spectacular extravagance. Yet that
title wouldn't do justice to the tyrannical
toughness with which he was prepared
to pursue his taste for luxury, or the
ruthlessness with which he was ready to
treat those who tried to stop him.

In 1293, he plunged his kingdom into
war with Edward I after confiscating the
English monarch's duchy of Aquitaine, in
southwestern France. When, four years
later, the northerly province of Flanders
(now in northern Belgium) sought to
secede, he launched a second – and once
more hugely expensive – war. When his
extravagance was condemned by Pope
Boniface VIII, Philip cunningly combined
a little sweet revenge with some good
housekeeping, imposing savage tax rises on
the clergy across his realm.

It would be wrong to dismiss Philip
the Fair as simply being self-indulgent.
In historical hindsight, he can be seen to
have started the construction of a strongly
centralized state in France, rather as Henry
V (1386–1422; reigned 1413–22) and his
Tudor line were to do in England. As it was
experienced by important groups among
his subjects, though, his was a wayward
autocracy, ruled with a 'whim of iron'.

Above: Philip IV, as imagined by an unknown
eighteenth-century painter at Versailles: he was,
of course, the Bourbons' kind of king.

That there was 'nothing personal' about
his persecution of groups like the Lombard
merchants in his country didn't make it any
less unpleasant. Deeply in debt to them, in
1293, rather than repay what he owed, he
extorted 250,000 livres from them in return
for the citizenship that would allow them
to remain within his realm. In 1306, he
expelled the Jews from France – earning his
country an entry in the history of European
antisemitism; a price worth paying for the
removal of so many pressing creditors.
Seen in this context, his attack on the
Knights Templar – to whom he also owed
a colossal amount of money – ceases to
seem in any way surprising.

Above: Philip couldn't have asked for a more obliging pope than Clement V.

The Knights Templar were of course in Philip's sights – not just as a potent (and potentially-threatening) political force but as a possible source of revenues, given their great wealth. This, at least, is the interpretation modern historians have mostly placed upon his actions against the Order. He avowed a more pure-hearted moral outrage:

A bitter thing, a lamentable thing, a thing which is horrible to contemplate, terrible to hear of, a detestable crime, an execrable evil, an abominable work … a thing almost inhuman, indeed set apart from all humanity has, thanks to the report of several trustworthy persons, reached our ears … causing us to tremble with violent horror …

The Templars, he told his courtiers in September 1307, *surpass unreasoning beasts in their astonishing bestiality, they expose themselves to all the supremely abominable crimes which even the sensuality of unreasoning beasts abhors and avoids. Not only by their acts and their detestable deeds, but even by their hasty words, they defile the earth with their filth, they undo the benefits of the dew, they corrupt the purity of the air and bring about the confusion of our faith.*

Grave – if unspecific – charges. Philip spelled out some of the detail in the weeks that followed. The Order wasn't just wicked but, quite literally, godless, he maintained. On joining, the young novice had to renounce Christ, deny his divinity and ceremonially spit upon his crucifix three times.

He also had to kiss his (male, of course) preceptor on the mouth, navel and spinal base – the Knights Templar were a set of sodomites, it was implied. And then, indeed, expressly stated: it was stipulated in the Order's regulations, Philip said, that the true Knight would be ready to submit to his comrades' sexual desires.

The initiate also had to acknowledge his willingness to worship the kind of 'graven images' outlawed by the biblical Ten Commandments (Exodus 20, 4), along with more exotic idols, including animals. The claim that the initiation ceremony was followed by a form of mass in which the Eucharistic host was left unconsecrated, so remained as bread, is more unfathomable, from our modern point of view, perhaps. But it can of course be seen as parodically inverting the idolatries and, in that sense, positing a sort of spiritual equivalence with them. This empty show of a service, without the central sacrament that justified it, struck the medieval mind as particularly blasphemous, it seems.

A CYNICAL SWOOP

Only the most exalted – and hence most egregiously wicked – of Templars got to witness the special ceremony at the centre of Philip's final charge. 'A man's head with a long beard', he said, was held up for special adoration. Those high-ranking Templar

BAPHOMET

THE HEAD HELD UP for worship (allegedly) at the most secret Templar meetings would appear to have been the Baphomet-idol referred to in some accounts of Templar ceremonies. The word is often assumed to be a corruption of the Islamic Prophet's name, Muhammad, but who can tell?

Some accounts, however, have Baphomet appearing as a black cat or other creature. The name came up at several points in the interrogation of Templar suspects during the Paris process, but there was no consistent agreement over what or who this deity or devil was. The picture has been further confused by Baphomet's subsequent adoption in a later occult tradition in which (often represented as a goat-headed figure) he derives his characteristics from a range of esoteric ancient gods.

ESQUIN DE FLOYRAN

A SERIOUSLY SHADOWY FIGURE, Esquin de Floryan flits into the historical record for just long enough to denounce the Order and then flits out again into oblivion. We don't have birth- or death dates for him, but he's believed to have been the prior of a Templar community at Montfaucon, near Limoges, before falling out with the Order for reasons which remain unclear.

Unless, that is, we choose to believe his claims to have been upset by the blasphemy, bestiality and sodomy systemically present in the Order, according to the testimony he took to King James II of Aragon (1267–1327; reigned 1291–1327) in 1305. James appears to have treated De Floryan's story with disdain, but he fared better with Philip the Fair a couple of years later.

Philip got his counsellor Guillaume de Nogaret (c. 1260–1313) to follow up his allegations. A twin-track approach of torture and bribery secured the necessary 'corroboration': the Templars' reputation was left in shreds.

officials present kissed and worshipped it at their secret chapter meetings, he insisted.

In a series of raids the length and breadth of France, on Friday 13 October 1307, Jacques de Molay, and anything up to 15,000 'Knights Templar', were arrested by Philip's men. As important: their lands and funds were confiscated by the Crown.

Below: Jacques de Molay is tortured by King Philip's men.

Actually, only a few hundred of those picked up were really 'knights', as such: most were lay officials, servants or tenant farmers. Any affiliation with the Order would do, it seemed. A number appear to have been nothing more than serfs who'd happened to be tied to Templar estates.

In isolation and abject terror, of course, the confessions came spilling out, confirming all the lurid horror stories. Severe torture helped coax the stronger to comply. Their bodies racked to breaking point; the bare soles of their feet burned or beaten; their teeth pulled out or their testicles flayed ... they were generally ready to acknowledge their guilt before too long.

As one commentator wrote a few months later:

The human tongue cannot express the punishment, afflictions, miseries, taunts, and dire kinds of torture suffered by the said innocents in the space of three months, since the day of their arrest, since by day and night constant sobs and sighs have not ceased in their cells, nor have cries and gnashing of teeth ceased in their tortures ... Truth kills them, and lies liberate them from death.

One subject on which those accused don't seem to have felt able to offer even liberating lies was that of sodomy, Gordon Napier points out in his history of the Templars. Only three of the 138 knights who were formally tried in Paris admitted to this particular offence – whereas 123 confessed to spitting on Christ's cross. That doesn't necessarily mean that it didn't happen: it does, however, suggest that it was so strongly taboo among the Templars that we might reasonably wonder how likely it is that it really did.

Below: The arrest of the Templars, as recorded in the fourteenth-century *Chroniques de France*.

READY TO BELIEVE

A secret show-trial would seem to be a contradiction in terms, and yet it's pretty much what Philip had contrived for the Knights Templar. If all interrogations took place in secrecy and darkness, their 'findings' – the more scurrilous the better – were broadcast far and wide, and immediately – months before the accused had seen the inside of any court.

In truth, the charges against the Knights appear to have been as laughable as James

Opposite: Philip the Fair
looks on as Templar
knights are burned.

Below: Portugal's Denis
I sympathized with the
Templars, and tried to
perpetuate their ideals.

of Aragon had clearly concluded, and Philip's acceptance of
the findings was only too obviously mischievous. That didn't
mean they didn't get traction, though: a lot of people in France
already felt that the Templars had grown too powerful and rich.
And, in the face of so sustained a barrage of propaganda on the
subject – including the revelation that confessions had been made
(however dubiously obtained) – many were ready to believe that
the king was right.

SPREADING THE NET

So outrageous was Philip's conduct
that even the supine Clement V
became concerned – especially as
the king claimed to be doing all this
in the Church's name. Despite this,
on the back of the 'evidence' that
France's torturers had been amassing,
that November Clement sent out the
order for a crackdown on the Knights
Templar in other realms. His bull,
Pastoralis praeeminentiae (November
1307), demanded that – as a matter
of religious duty – Europe's monarchs
should arrest and prosecute the
Templars in their countries.

Not all were convinced, by any
means. England's Edward II (1284–
1327; reigned 1307–27) confessed
himself 'unable to credit the horrible
charges against the Knights Templar,
who everywhere bear a good name
in England'. He sent letters in their
support to the kings of Portugal,
Castile, Aragon and Sicily. To a
greater or a lesser extent, they seem
to have shared Edward's misgivings,
though reluctant to defy the direct

RANK OUTSIDERS

IT MIGHT PRIDE ITSELF on being 'first with the news', but the world's mass media doesn't always move quite so quickly. In 2014, it revealed that a village in central France had gloried in the name 'Mort-aux-Juifs' ('Death to the Jews') since the fourteenth century. It was newsworthy now because pleas from the Simon Wiesenthal Foundation to have it changed were being furiously resisted, on the grounds of 'history' and 'heritage'. Scholarly suggestions that the name was the corruption of the medieval *maret* ('marsh') of *juin* (an old word for 'manure' or simply 'muck') were brushed aside – and rightly so, because it was the modern, antisemitic version to which villagers were so staunchly attached.

How much hatred of the Jews had actually existed in the 1300s, it's hard to say for sure. The pseudoscientific racial philosophies of the nineteenth and twentieth centuries were obviously as yet a long way off. The assumption that the Jews were eternally cursed as 'Christ-Killers' was well embedded, though; as was acceptance of the so-called 'Blood Libel' – the claim that the Jews abducted Christian children to use their blood in making their unleavened bread. Then as now, such prejudices were to some extent born of sheer, doltish ignorance; then as now they were fomented by those with an interest in increasing strife.

In 1306, quite obviously, the man with the most obvious interest was King Philip – who helped himself to the property of his kingdom's excluded Jews.

Anti-Templar feeling wasn't so different from the suspicion and hostility traditionally felt towards the Jews. The Order's reputed wealth was resented, as was the power the Templars appeared to wield as moneylenders. Everyone loves a conspiracy theory and, again, as with the Jews, the Templars' very separateness – and the secrecy surrounding them – seemed to license speculation. Philip's first motivation may have been financial, but it made as much sense for him to attack the Templars as it had to go for the Jews (and, earlier, the Lombards): all were envied and feared as wealthy and clannish outsider groups.

commandment of the Pope. James II of Aragon had made his scepticism as to the claims against the Templars very clear. Denis of Portugal (1261–1325; reigned 1279–1325) was a few years later (1319) to found his own military order, the Order of Christ, which actually included several surviving former Knights Templar.

Ferdinand IV of Castile (1285–1312; reigned 1295–1312) was more cooperative. But then he was subsequently to be remembered as 'Ferdinand the Summoned', after the story that Jacques de Molay cursed him to be called before a hellish judgment when he died. It was hard, in fairness, for a medieval monarch to stand out against his Pope on a religious issue – harder than even Catholic believers today could understand, perhaps. Ferdinand was unusual only in his alacrity in falling into line: his fellow rulers – even Edward II – would submit in time.

> IT WAS HARD FOR A MEDIEVAL MONARCH TO HOLD OUT AGAINST HIS POPE.

'DILIGENTLY EXAMINED BY US …'

There were mixed signals within the Church as well. In 1308, for instance, Pope Clement had the leading defendants brought up before a panel of his own, so he could establish the 'pure, complete and uncompromised truth' of what had been done from the accused. Three of his leading cardinals were present, along with an impressive array of witnesses, notaries and other officials, at the castle at Chinon, Indre-et-Loire, where Jacques de Molay and his brethren were being held.

The so-called 'Chinon Parchment' records the proceedings in some detail. It was discovered by Barbara Frale, in the Vatican's Secret Archives (a real place, and an official title), in 2001. All the accustomed charges are rehearsed, and all the French court's guilty findings more or less refuted. Some ambiguity does emerge around the 'spitting on the cross' and 'denial of Christ' components of the initiation ceremony: such demands may have been made as a sort of ritualistic 'test', it's been suggested.

Clement's commission certainly had no hesitation in absolving the accused of any serious wrongdoing. Principle was trumped by politics, though, and any moral courage Clement may have had

by his fear of Philip, whose hardline stance was buttressed by his forced 'confessions'. August as it nominally was, then, this new judgment was swept aside, and august as he nominally was, Pope Clement meekly accepted this.

Some within the Church were evidently only too happy for this result to stand. Archbishop Burchard III (?–1235; in office 1307–27) of Magdeburg comes across as having been a

Above: The so-called 'Chinon Parchment' gives chapter and verse on the case against the Knights Templar – and the paucity of 'evidence' against them.

Above: Out of loyalty to Philip, Pope Clement tried hard to see the Templars as heretical, but could at best only convict them of the odd mistake.

sort of small-time Philip IV. A longstanding foe of the Knights Templar, he had several burned at the stake in his archdiocese, and confiscated the Order's property. Elsewhere in Germany, at Mainz and Triers, for instance, tribunals acquitted Templar defendants on all charges. A trial in Edinburgh, Scotland, ended the same way.

Pope Clement gave what feeble backing he felt he could to the Templars' pleas for a proper, public trial to be held in France. But Philip was determined not to be diverted from his course. In May 1310, he had 54 Knights Templar burned at the stake in Paris. Essentially a cruel stunt, this action was clearly intended to impress the people with the perilousness of the situation France was facing. And, of course, to dispose of inconvenient potential witnesses for the defence should proceedings ever see the light of day.

CLEMENT COLLAPSES

So events limped on: in March 1312, Pope Clement issued his bull *Vox in Excelso* ('Voice in the Highest'). 'In view of the suspicion, infamy, loud insinuations and other things' advanced against the Knights Templar, he says, and of the 'serious scandal' that had accompanied these claims, he had no alternative but to suppress the Order, 'by an irrevocable and perpetually valid decree'.

So far, so much a study in the art of weaving weasel words into a tapestry of seeming truth: it's the scandal voiced about the Order that demands its abolition, not its actual deeds. In fairness, Clement did screw up his courage to come out with an actual and explicit lie in his reference to the 'many horrible things which have been done by the very many of the brothers of this Order, who have lapsed into the sin of wicked apostasy, the crime of detestable idolatry, and the execrable outrage of the Sodomites.' His own commission, a couple of years before, had considered these charges and firmly rejected them. Still, in the circumstances, what was a pope to do?

Simply double down, it seems. A couple of months later, Clement published another bull, *Ad providam* ('For the Provision'), which ordered that all Knights Templar property should be confiscated and made over to the Knights Hospitaller.

BURNT OFFERING

Jacques de Molay had confessed under torture fairly quickly, we've seen; so too had his henchman Geoffroi de Charney (?–1314). Their supposed honesty and penitence earned them the mercy of the Church. And, consequently, an indefinite prison sentence – though at the same time it spared them their lives. For the penalty for heresy was always death.

Below: Jacques de Molay and Geoffroi de Charney go to their deaths, 1314.

On 18 March 1314, paraded on a platform in front of the cathedral of Notre Dame in Paris, De Molay and De Charney were publicly condemned to spend the rest of their lives in prison. While the other knights arraigned alongside them accepted their sentences, the two top Templars, now apparently tiring of the pantomime, formally recanted the confessions they had made. They had, they said, offended only in lying about the Order's conduct, lending credit to others' slanders – in this alone, they insisted, had they sinned.

In the topsy-turvy world of the medieval Church – thrown into yet more confusion by Philip's bullying – that amounted to a re-embracing of their 'heretical' beliefs and practices. They were condemned to death on the spot; a pyre was built for them and they were burned.

THE TWO TOP TEMPLARS FORMALLY RECANTED THE CONFESSIONS THEY HAD MADE.

A DOUBTFUL INHERITANCE

Any early competition between the Knights Templar and Knights Hospitaller appears to have been largely forgotten some time since. In so far as it *had* endured, the Hospitallers had now clearly won. Not only had they outlasted their rivals, they had cleaned up on their forfeited power and wealth. Yet it wasn't to be quite so simple, it was soon clear.

As we've seen, *Ad providam* had in principle transferred all the Templars' property to the Knights Hospitaller. Obviously, though, this hadn't been how it all worked out in France. The whole point of Philip the Fair's campaign against the Knights Templar, after all, had been to get his hands on their extensive assets in the country.

Better-behaved monarchs do appear to have taken more trouble to give the Knights Hospitaller what was supposed to be theirs, though, as historian Helen Nicholson has pointed out, the temptation to hold on to at least some of this wealth themselves did get the better of several kings and leading nobles.

In certain cases, estates and other assets were reclaimed by members of those families whose ancestors had originally bestowed them on the Templars, but could now claim that, in

A MARTYR'S MALEDICTION

As THE FLAMES ROSE up around him, awestruck eyewitnesses were later to recall, Jacques de Molay passed his own judgment on the king and Clement – and on leading supporters such as Ferdinand IV of Castile. They'd meet again, within the year, the Grand Master maintained, before the throne of an angry God on high.

Ferdinand was already dead by then, so De Molay didn't risk anything by naming him. It's quite true, though, that Clement V would be gone within a month. The church where his body lay in state was struck by lightning and burned down, effectively cremating him. As for Philip, he had a stroke that same November while out hunting in the woods near Pont-Sainte-Maxence, north of Paris. Within a few weeks he had died as well.

Below: England's Edward II moved against the English Templars only with immense reluctance. Eventually, though, he did bring them to trial.

the absence of any such order, the properties were rightfully theirs once more. They weren't necessarily motivated by the desire for gain: often what was taken back was quickly re-gifted to other orders or institutions. All too often, moreover, when the Hospitallers did receive some former Templar property, it

Right: A Templar (left) and Hospitaller knight occupy adjacent windows in Warwickshire's Church of St Andrew, Temple Grafton.

came to them encumbered with debts or other liabilities. Amid the paranoid politicking of their last few tumultuous years, the Knights Templar hadn't necessarily given estate-management the attention they might have done.

In any case, the Knights Hospitaller's expenses at this time were quite enormous. The three-year Siege of Rhodes had not come cheap. Nor did their subsequent efforts to secure their hold on their new island stronghold. The construction of fortifications here was to continue well into the fifteenth century. Already, though, their outgoings were immense.

So too were the costs of creating a naval fighting force virtually from scratch – though the new fleet at least showed signs of earning its own keep. No operation remotely worthy of being described as a 'crusade' was undertaken, or even envisaged, during this period, but the

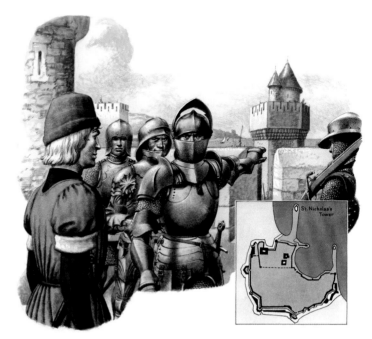

Below: The Knights Hospitaller's headquarters in Rhodes.

ST THOMAS 'TROUBLES'

WHILE THE TEMPLARS WERE going out with a bang, the Knights of St Thomas went with a whimper. They'd been in gradual decline ever since the fall of Acre.

At that point, along with the rest of the crusading rump, they'd relocated to Cyprus, where, in Nicosia, they'd built the beautiful church of St Nicholas. (Though this was to be adapted for use as a market in the Ottoman era.) Bowing to the new realities, the Order stepped away from the military struggle and dedicated itself exclusively to crusade-related charitable works. Its internal politics – specifically bickering between the Knights in Cyprus and back 'home' in London – ensured its slide into increasing irrelevance and, ultimately, financial ruin, though it was to limp on, little more than a shell, till the sixteenth century.

Hospitallers still stopped and seized shipping from the Muslim world. They helped themselves to the vessels and their cargoes and ransomed important passengers.

ISLAND WAR

The category 'shipping from the Muslim world' could of course include vessels from Christian states, trading with the Turks and with Mamluk Egypt hence a string of Hospitaller attacks upon ships from Genoa. When, in 1311, merchants from that city demanded the return of several captured vessels, the Genoese approached Mesud (?–1319; reigned c. 1282–1319), the bey (or Turkish governor) of Menteshe, in southwest Anatolia, seeking naval support against the Knights Hospitaller.

After a sporadic series of small-scale attacks around the Aegean, the fighting escalated into full-on fighting at the Battle of Amorgos (1312). The Knights surprised the enemy while they were ashore on the island (the easternmost of the Cyclades group), burning 23 of their ships before landing themselves to do battle with the Turkish crews. The Hospitallers took severe casualties, but inflicted even greater ones: up to 800 Turkish sailors and soldiers were reported killed.

THE HOSPITALLERS TOOK SEVERE CASUALTIES BUT INFLICTED EVEN GREATER ONES.

Seven years later, it was the turn of the Aydinids to do battle on the Turkish side. This up-and-coming corsair dynasty had its base in the *beylik* of Aydin, on Anatolia's far west coast. Its founding father Mehmed Bey (?–1334; reigned 1308–34) had expanded the *beylik*'s territory by capturing the major port of Ephesus, further to the south; it was from here that he set out at the head of his own fleet to find the Knights Hospitaller.

He caught up with them off the island of Chios, but must very quickly have wished he hadn't: a good two thirds of his fleet was sunk in the ensuing fray. But Mehmed Bey was a patient man: under himself and his successors, the Aydinid Dynasty was to emerge as the dominant naval power in the Aegean.

As the Aydinids grew in power, they became an ever more potent threat to Christian shipping in the region; their attacks a steady drain on what should have been the profits of western

SUBTLETY AND SPEED: THE GALLEY

WARSHIPS IN THE MEDIEVAL Mediterranean were constructed in the *galia sottile* style. As the Italian name (literally 'slender galley') suggests, they were long (around 40m (130ft), typically) and narrow (maybe 5–6m (16–20ft)

Above: Galleys like this one carried the Crusaders into war.

in the beam). They must have been very beautiful – if not to the enemy on whom they were bearing down at terrifying speed, thanks to their banks of driving oars.

Rowed vessels, like the longship of the Vikings, had been going out of use in the Atlantic. In the comparative calm of the Mediterranean, though, oar power remained perfectly practical; indeed, the changeable winds here made it a real boon. Among the Aegean islands, especially, sea-spaces were confined: the galley's speed over short distances was invaluable.

The medieval galley had much in common with those in use in classical antiquity. There were important differences, even so. The strengthened prow with waterline-level ram was gone: galleys might now bump and jostle one another to knock opposing crews off-balance and facilitate boarding, but they weren't the charging, smashing machines they once had been.

The simple steering oar that Homer's heroes would have used had evolved over centuries into a rudimentary 'quarter-rudder'. Like the ancient oar, however, this was mounted on the side of the vessel, well aft, rather than behind on the stern itself. Greek and Roman navigators would also have been surprised to see the triangular *lateen* sail – often two – which had crept into use under Arab influence in the Middle Ages.

The rowers sat on benches, between one and three to an oar, and raised up on their own special platform so they wouldn't impede the work of the remaining crew. They don't seem to have been slaves or convicts – that was to be a later development – but were trained to fight as soldiers as required.

trade. Concerted campaigns were fought against them, then, the Knights Hospitaller joining forces with an assortment of Christian states so as to be able to match the strength of the Aydinids' now-formidable naval fleet. While often enjoying papal backing, these various naval leagues were generally assembled

Right: The Hospitallers do battle off Episkopi, Cyprus, 1323 (a painting by Auguste Etienne Francois Mayer, 1841).

with the most materialistic of motives. Christian Europe wanted its mercantile traffic to flow freely and lucratively, untroubled by the Turks.

In 1333, a fleet was put together by the Knights Hospitaller and the Republic of Venice to resist a new threat, that of the

northwestern Anatolian *beylik* of Karasi. Ten ships each from the Hospitallers and the Venetians, together with a further fourteen from France, the Papal States and Cyprus, added up to a fairly impressive fleet. In the autumn of 1334, the Gulf of Adramyttium (off what is now known as Edremit) was the scene of a spectacular victory for the 'Crusaders'. As many as 200 ships were said to have been sunk, and several thousand Turkish sailors killed.

CLEMENT'S CRUSADE

The Battle of Adramyttium was arguably a sideshow (albeit an impressive one) to what have become known as the Smyrniote Crusades (1344–51) because they took as their target Smyrna – or Izmir, as it's now called. This ancient seaport had become a headquarters for the Aydinids, by now the Christians' naval nemesis, under the rule of Umur Bey (c. 1309–48; reigned 1334–48), an admiral of real flair.

They rejoiced in the title of 'Crusades' because they had been called for by Pope Clement VI (1291–1362; reigned 1342–52). The fourth of the Avignon Popes, Clement was a patriotic Frenchman, who favoured his country's king, Philip VI (1293–1350; reigned 1328–50), in many ways. But he was in no doubt of his duty to defend his faith – militarily, if necessary. Half a century after the Fall of Acre, at a time when so many others had been moving on, he remained romantically committed to the crusading ideal.

Its opening engagement came with the Battle of Pallene (May, 1344). This was fought off the promontory of that name, the westernmost of three extending south- and eastward from the end of the Chalkidiki peninsula, Macedonia, in northern Greece. Ships from the Papal States, Venice and Cyprus joined with those of the Knights Hospitaller – even so, this combined Christian fleet had only 24 vessels to the 60 of the Turks'.

Despite these adverse odds, the Christian galleys outmanoeuvred the enemy, cornering them in an inlet off what is now the village of Sykia, Sithonia. There they set fire to the Turkish vessels as their terrified crews streamed ashore in headlong flight. No fewer than 52 ships were destroyed.

AS MANY AS 200 SHIPS WERE SAID TO HAVE BEEN SUNK.

Left: Clement VI is boiled in a cauldron in a hostile caricature. The cock (Latin gallus – so 'gallic') reflects his close allegiance to his native France.

SMYRNA STALEMATE

The crusading fleet then made its way to Smyrna, where a few months later it landed, occupied the harbour and much of the city itself before laying siege to the citadel, whose Turkish garrison was ready to defend it to the death.

As Turkish reinforcements then arrived, a siege-within-a-siege ensued, but the Crusaders managed to hang on by their fingernails for the following two years. Indeed, it was not until May 1347 that a Knights Hospitaller-led relief expedition won its way through to relieve them. To do so, it had to defeat a much larger Turkish fleet off the island of Imbros. An impressive victory – but one that even so could secure only partial fulfilment for the crusading project. The Christians could hold on only to their foothold in the lower city, round Smyrna's port.

By 1351, Clement's health was failing fast – and with it his interest in the crusade he'd called. Despite this, Christian forces were to hang on here for a full half-century after, resisting every effort by the Turks to dislodge them. This was another impressive – if for the most part unsung – triumph. Again, though, it was one that brought no appreciable gain to the western cause – galling as it must have been for the Turks.

Below: The French Romantic artist Henri Delaborde painted this scene in which the Knights Hospitaller recover Armenia for Christianity.

ALEXANDRIAN OUTRAGE

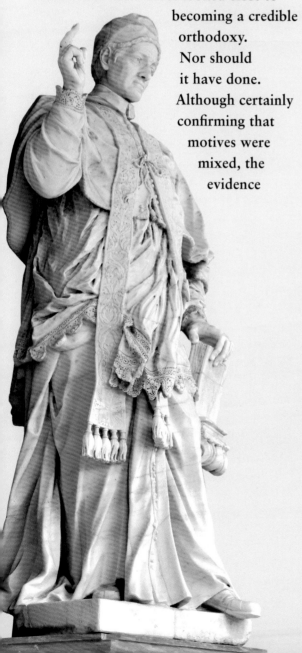

THOSE MODERN COMMENTATORS WHO denounced the Crusades as rapacious, proto-colonial adventures have had to settle for 'gadfly' status in recent years. Sceptical revisionism is never wasted, perhaps, but this arguably self-lacerating anti-western view never looked close to becoming a credible orthodoxy. Nor should it have done. Although certainly confirming that motives were mixed, the evidence falls far short of backing the view that the whole crusading project was an opportunistic sham.

But then the Alexandrian Crusade comes along: the egregious exception that seems to prove the cynics' point. It took place in 1365, under the leadership of Peter I of Cyprus (1328–69; reigned 1358–69). It was nevertheless a real crusade, though, blessed as it was by no less a personage than Pope Urban V (1310–70; reigned 1362–70). Europe's leading princes lined up to praise Peter's piety and courage in taking on the Mamluks.

Setting sail from Venice in June 1365 with over 160 ships, he voyaged to Egypt via Rhodes. There his fleet was augmented by a Knights Hospitaller squadron. They sailed on together to Alexandria reaching that great port on about 9 October and finding it only scantily defended. So Peter and his soldiers spent three whole days and nights roaming through the city, burning, looting and killing. At least 20,000 men, women and children appear to have been slaughtered. Some 70 ships were loaded up with booty – which included 5000 people carried off as slaves. At this point, a Mamluk army approaching, the 'Crusaders' deemed discretion the better part of valour. They climbed back aboard their ships and sailed off again.

Left: Urban V may have given the Alexandrian Crusade his blessing, but – pope or not – that couldn't make it right.

6

SIEGE MENTALITY

The fifteenth century brought some spectacular successes for the military orders. But the world they had been founded for was disappearing.

THROUGH THE second half of June and on through July, an edgy, unsettling stalemate held: the heat of the dog days only heightened the itchy sense of inconclusiveness both sides felt. There was to be no lazy summer at the Siege of Rhodes. The net totality might be immovable torpor, but activity was frantic and unceasing, the scene one of scurrying urgency and haste.

SLUGGING IT OUT

While the defenders dug in as best they could, the attackers built their own offensive earthworks under thunderous covering fire from eight great cannon. Inside the city, the Knights Hospitaller and their Christian supporters built massive catapults to hurl huge stones down on the Turks beneath. Grand Master Pierre

Opposite: Pierre d'Aubusson pays a visit to his troops on the fortifications of Rhodes, from an edition of Guillaume Caoursin's *Relation du sieège de Rhodes.*

d'Aubusson (1423–1503; in office 1476–1503) had also had the Hospitallers' own bombard – a sort of giant mortar – cast. Even so, the Ottoman enemy continued to toil, slowly but inexorably raising ramps. First filling in the defensive ditch beneath the walls, these inched upward day by day, bringing the battlements above within ever closer reach.

The Christians set up projecting spars of timber to keep scaling ladders at a distance; they hung out woven mats of reed and twig to buffer the bare masonry against the shock of cannonballs. Along their walkways atop the walls, preparing against the worst, they piled up casks of tar, gunpowder and sulphur, which could be set alight at a moment's notice. The Turks replied with words, shooting letters in over the walls with arrows. They offered mercy to those who surrendered, impalement to those who didn't. (They had 8000 stakes sharpened in readiness, they claimed.) Those inside the city knew the attackers were trying to sow division between its Latin occupants and local Greeks, but that didn't make the messages any less alarming.

Days and days, and weeks and weeks went by without a breakthrough on either side. Temperatures dropped, but patience too was dwindling. By November, the Ottoman commander Mesih Pasha (?–1501) was getting tired of waiting. As the month approached its end, he told his officers it was time to strike. On the 27th, the eve of the day he had appointed for this attack, the Turks called on Allah for his assistance in the coming battle. They washed their bodies in ritual readiness for the fray.

Meanwhile their gunners stepped up their bombardment of the city walls. In many places, these had already been reduced to rubble. Ironically, now, they were likely to prove less of an obstacle to the Turks from the tops of their attacking ramps than they were to the defenders they were meant to be protecting. They would have to clamber up the slopes of debris from street level inside the city to reach their positions.

INTO ACTION

On the morning of Friday 28 November, a shot from a mortar gave the signal for the final assault. A wave of 2500 shock-troops surged forward, and took possession of the walls. Turkish troops streamed after them in overwhelming numbers – perhaps as many as 20,000 more. It was almost a miracle that the Knights Hospitaller didn't simply fold in the face of such a tsunami of hostile strength. There were 250 of them, and while they were backed by 2–3000 local militiamen and mercenaries, they were hopelessly outnumbered nonetheless.

But they didn't fold. Instead, having paused to rally, they hit back heroically. Down, but still by no means out, they rushed forward themselves, sweeping wide to outflank the leading Turks and corral them in the confined spaces of the wall-top walkways. Several hundred of the attackers were hurled down from here into the streets below, where exulting enemies cut them limb from limb. Brave as they were, though, the Knights were beaten: the odds they faced just too impossible for them to hope for anything better than death with honour.

Opposite top: The Hospitallers' Grand Master at the Siege of Rhodes, Pierre d'Aubusson.

Opposite bottom: Mesih Pasha.

Below: The Turkish fleet advances upon Rhodes for the Siege of 1480, from a fifteenth-century manuscript.

They were prepared to buy that honour with their lives, and uphold their faith even in their dying moments. Even as the triumphant Turks raised their gold- and silver-streamered standard on the walls of Rhodes, they countered, raising a richly embroidered banner of their own. At its centre, Christ hung on his cross, between the figures of John the Baptist and the Virgin Mary.

A BLAZING CROSS OF GOLD LIT UP THE VAST AND BILLOWING CLOUDS.

A splendid sight – but impressive as the banner was, it prompted a more spectacular vision by far in the skies above. Not for the Christian defenders themselves, however. It was, we're told by the Hospitaller Guillaume Caoursin (1430–1501), who chronicled these events, the Turks who looked up incredulously to see a huge heavenly reflection of the standard on the walls below.

A blazing cross of gold lit up the vast and billowing clouds. Beside it, on one side, stood the Blessed Virgin Mary, Queen of Heaven. Her gown aglow in dazzling white, she bore a resplendent shield in her left hand; with the right she raised a long, sharp, twinkling spear of war aloft. On the other side of the cross, a man in 'vile raiment' – St John the Baptist in his desert garb of skins and camel-hair – came backed by a throng of knights in gleaming armour, marching in across the sky to save the city.

Terrified, the Turks broke ranks and ran. Their army was no match for this airy host. With the assistance of these heaven-sent reinforcements, the Knights Hospitaller had won the day. Mesih was sent packing with his invasion force.

STARTING GUN

Opposite: Turkish commanders discuss their next move, in hope of breaking the enduring deadlock, from an edition of Guillaume Caoursin's *Relation du siège de Rhodes*.

Quite some *son et lumière* ... but was this spectacular conclusion to 1480's Siege of Rhodes also a grand finale to the Age of Faith? We may of course wonder why the Turks, who are supposed to have experienced it, didn't think to mention it in their reports of the battle. Too embarrassed, Caoursin would presumably have argued, to dwell on a defeat that didn't just expose their military shortcomings but crucial shortcomings in their faith as well.

It's striking even so how important elements of religious ritual are to both sides here (the Ottomans' ablutions; the Hospitallers' banner) even before the heavenly company makes its entrance. On the other, there are those elements that haven't previously appeared in our historical narrative before – most notably the use of mortars and cannon by both sides.

Prior to the opportune arrival of Our Lady's airborne army, cannon-fire had levelled large stretches of the city walls. The military architecture of many centuries was suddenly obsolete. So, it seemed, were all manner of medieval assumptions and attitudes. An expansion in scientific knowledge was beginning to bring with it an expansion in technology, which in its turn was bound to impact on the wider culture.

Above: A Turkish cannon from the time of the Siege of Rhodes. For portability, it could be unscrewed into two sections.

Some scholars date the start of the Renaissance to as far back as the thirteenth century, with the masterfully ambitious *Divine Comedy* of Dante (1265–1321). Or the fourteenth – when the lyrical canzone of his fellow Italian poet Petrarch (1304–74) pointed the way to a new expressive confidence soon to be taken up by painters and sculptors. Suffice it to say that, at the time the Siege of Rhodes was going on, Florence's extraordinary artistic impresario Lorenzo de' Medici (1449–92) was 31, and, it is said, hosting a young artist named Leonardo da Vinci (1452–1519) in his home.

Cannon aren't canzone, of course, but both can be seen as representing the sort of can-do spirit now manifested in everything from medicine to sculpture, and from philosophy to navigation. Renaissance 'humanism' didn't dispense with the idea of God, but it did believe in the just about infinite capabilities of humankind.

Baldwin IV, we can easily imagine, wouldn't have been too taken aback at the heavenly vision seen at Rhodes. God was all-powerful: what prodigy could possibly be beyond him? But we can't imagine a Christian commander of the fifteenth century so pious that he'd pull his army up to offer prayers – casually discarding the advantage of surprise in doing so – as Baldwin had three hundred years before at Montgisard.

Nor, in the age of firearms, could there be much more than a ceremonial place for the knight-at-arms, bravely as the Hospitallers had fought at Rhodes. The great age of chivalry already lay some distance in the past. If the military orders still had an undoubted glamour, there was a nostalgic air about them; they seemed not so much real soldiers now as figures of romance.

POWER IN PRUSSIA

Not that there had been anything unreal about the state the Teutonic Knights had presided over in Prussia through much of the fourteenth century and on into the early decades of the fifteenth. Difficult as it had been to carve out their colony here, they'd gradually tightened their hold over this territory and its pagan population – now successfully Christianized.

Below: The Jagiellonian Dynasty's founding couple, Jogailo and Jadwiga.

Indeed, when a threat to their authority finally came at the beginning of the fifteenth century, it was from the Catholic rulers of the combined kingdom of Poland and Lithuania. Grand Duke Wladyslaw II Jagiello, or 'Jogailo', of Lithuania (c. 1355–1434; reigned 1377–1434) had been brought up a pagan, but had converted so as to be able to marry Poland's Princess Jadwiga (c. 1373–99) in 1386. Well 'worth a mass', this marriage had made him master of both realms. Jogailo had by the 1390s extended his authority as far south as Transylvania and Moldavia (now Moldova), east to Moscow and west as far as Silesia and founded a powerful line of 'Jagiellonian' kings.

TRAGEDY AT TANNENBERG

A collision between the Teutonic Knights and this upstart state of Slavs was becoming all but inevitable. Jogailo made no secret of the fact that he was fomenting unrest against the Order. Something had to give, and on 15 July 1410, opposing forces met at Grunwald (also known as Tannenberg), now in northern Poland. Anything up to 20,000 Knights lined up against a still greater force of Jagiellonian cavalry. 'The forces of the Polish King were so numerous that there is no number high enough in the human language,' the *Prussian Chronicle* claimed – though

Below: A patriotic Polish interpretation (by the nineteenth-century painter Jan Matejko) on the Teutonic Knights' devastating loss at Grunwald, 1410.

modern scholarship has estimated 30,000. Both sides had thousands of infantrymen, crossbowmen and archers as well, making this one of the biggest battles of the medieval age.

Moving with the times, the Teutonic Knights had field artillery, too. So optimistic were they about the advantage it would give them that they kept many of their cavalry in reserve. In the event, rain doused their powder, and they found themselves caught short. When news came in at this crisis point that their Grand Master, Ulrich von Jungingen (c. 1360–1410), had been killed, morale collapsed; they broke and fled in disarray.

Between its devastating losses in the field itself, and the fortune it had to hand over afterwards to ransom thousands of prisoners, the Order was brought to the brink of complete collapse. Though ostensibly as powerful as ever (they held on to all their territories in Prussia), the Teutonic Knights were no longer really feared.

They were hated though – the more so because, in an attempt to offset their financial problems, they imposed excessive taxes across their state. By the middle of the century, a relatively strong and wilful local aristocracy had emerged across the country, along with the beginnings of a middle class in Prussia's towns. In 1454, this class rose up, leading a wider popular uprising against the Knights. They put it down, but only after 13 years and at enormous cost.

DANZIG DESTROYED

ANY DOUBT THAT THE Teutonic Knights were capable of acting with the utmost cynicism and greed had been dispelled by their conquest of Danzig in 1308. They'd actually been invited to the Baltic port (now Polish Gdansk) by the local governor, known only as Bogusza, who administered it on behalf of King Wladyslaw I 'the Elbow-High' (c. 1260–1333; reigned 1306–33).

This whole northern region, including Pomeralia and Brandenburg, had yet to accept King Wladyslaw's rule – or its absorption into a greater Poland in the first place. Now, a group of nobles had actually risen up in rebellion and advanced on the area's administrative capital. With Wladyslaw himself fully occupied putting down a revolt in the south of his unruly realm, Bogusza called the Teutonic Order in. Under the command of Heinrich von Plötzke (c. 1264–1320) they quickly – and

brutally – lifted the siege. Polish–German relations have been strained on and off pretty much ever since, so it's hard to be sure of the scale of the 'Gdansk Massacre'. No one disputes that the Knights went in hard on the rebels or that the dead and dying were left littering the city's streets, but there's not even the least approximation of a consensus on the death toll. Patriotic Polish historians have claimed that as many as 10,000 were slaughtered – all but unbelievable: the biggest medieval 'cities' were by modern standards small. Some sceptical scholars have suggested casualties of only a few score – and certainly below the hundred mark. Really, though, it's impossible to know.

Afterwards, when Wladyslaw, now back from his travels, refused to meet their terms, the Teutonic Knights set survivors to levelling their own town.

Above: João I of Portugal in (perhaps hypocritical) pious posture.

Below: João I, Grand Master of the Order of Aviz, leads his outnumbered forces to victory over Castile at Aljubarrota.

In Portugal, meanwhile, the Order of Aviz had just won itself an important (if arguably unethical) political breakthrough thanks to the ascension to the throne of King João I (1357–1433; reigned 1385–1433). As the illegitimate son of Pedro I (1320–67; reigned 1357–67), by his mistress Teresa Lourenço (c. 1330–?), a Lisbon merchant's daughter, he'd never been his father's official heir. His appointment, in 1364, as the Grand Master of Knights of Aviz, appears to have been meant as no more than a consolation prize.

KINGMAKERS

An incautious gesture, as things turned out – though not till two decades later, when Pedro's (legitimate) son and successor, Ferdinand I (1345–83; reigned 1367–83) died without a male heir. He did leave a wife, Leonor Teles (c. 1350–c.1405), and she was more than capable of acting as a regent to their daughter Beatriz (1373–c. 1420).

But Beatriz's marriage to Juan I of Castile (1358–90; reigned 1379–90) was (quite properly) perceived as a threat to Portuguese independence. How far he was motivated by

ANCHORING AUTHORITY

As the Christian monarchs pushed back the Moors in Spain, they found themselves in possession of a near-infinity of nothing much. Large areas of the interior were empty, undeveloped wastes. Such populations as they'd once had were long gone, dispersed by decades – if not centuries – of war. The Order of Calatrava came into its own in bringing regimentation to what had been a lawless void, creating Christian colonies in what had been No Man's Land.

As knights, they were well equipped to hold and where necessary fortify these newly conquered territories; they also had the organizational capacity to put the land to work. Through their own officials, or through tenant-farmers, they fostered an agricultural revolution, bringing more fertile valleys into arable production and opening up huge upland areas to grazing. In the province of Castilla-La Mancha, for instance, the Order had 'commanderies' round Malegón and Bolaños de Calatrava, in Ciudad Real, and in Vállaga, Guadalajara. By the end of the fourteenth century, the Knights had the stewardship of over 15,000 sq km (5800 sq miles) in Castile alone: 100,000 vassals worked their 50 commanderies.

The practice continued over successive centuries as the Reconquista pushed ever southward. Hence the establishment of a number of foundations in Castell de Castells, Valencia, in the thirteenth century.

In the south in the area between Córdoba and Jaén, Juan II (1405–54; reigned 1406–54) made extensive grants to the Order in Alto Guadalquivir: at Porcuna and Torredonjimeno, for example. And, in what must have struck the king as an enjoyable irony, at Martos, scene of a disastrous defeat for the Order at the hands of the Moors in 1275. Historically, then, the Order of Calatrava played a crucial role, not just in the military reconquest, but in the administrative and economic development of early-modern Spain.

Below: The final expulsion of the Moors from Spain, 1609.

patriotism and how far by personal ambition isn't clear, but João I led a campaign of resistance to Beatriz. And, thanks to his function of Grand Master to the Order of Aviz, he had what amounted to a private army at his back.

Things took a turn for the sensational in December 1383, when he and some knightly companions murdered Juan Fernández Andeiro (c. 1320–83). The Galician count was an important protector to the Regent and was rumoured to have been her lover. Leonor herself was then driven from her country, seeking refuge with – and support from – her son-in-law. In April, 1385, as João I received the recognition of Portugal's Cortes as king, Juan I led an invading army across the border. But they were badly beaten by João and his knights at the Battle of Aljubarrota.

EMPIRE BUILDERS

The dynasty João founded was to become known as the House of Aviz and was to dominate Portugal until the end of the sixteenth century. João's fourth son Henrique (1394–1460) – 'Prince Henry the Navigator', as he's known in English – may not have been destined to reign himself, but the voyages of discovery he sponsored set Portugal off along the road to empire.

The first step along that road had, however, already been taken by Henrique's elder brother, King Duarte (1391–1438; reigned 1433–8). Just a short hop away from Spain across the Straits of Gibraltar on the North African coast, Ceuta had been a launching point for the Moorish invasion of Iberia, seven centuries before. There was a convincing crusading logic, then, in Duarte's decision to take the Moroccan city in a surprise attack by sea in August 1415 – even if his real motives were almost certainly more worldly. Ceuta's capture didn't just give Portugal a colonial foothold

Below: Not yet 'The Navigator', Prince Henry saw action at the Conquest of Ceuta as a young man.

PRINCE HENRY
OF
PORTUGAIL

CEUTA

Below: The fight for
Tangier, as recorded (with
perhaps more dignity
than the episode really
warranted) by
the makers of a
Portuguese tapestry.

in another continent: it showed an intent to take the Christian Reconquista to the very homeland of the Moors.

A fleet 200 vessels strong landed 45,000 men on the coast outside the city. The attack was led, of course, by the Order of Aviz. 'You may imagine the ardour of the combatants on both sides,' wrote the chronicler Gomes Eannes de Azurara (c. 1410–74); 'The din of battle was so great that there were

THE HOLY PRINCE

João's youngest son, the Infante Ferdinand (1402–43), was known as the 'Holy Prince'. His health was never of the most robust, and he grew up in comparative retirement.

Shy and timid, he was drawn to the religious life, though he was never to take orders.

Even so, in 1434, he took up the position of lay administrator to the Order of Aviz. And, in 1437, he signed himself and his knights up to his brother Henrique's expedition to Tangier – which the Prince intended to take from Morocco's Marinid rulers. To Ferdinand, this wasn't just an adventure but could be seen as a crusade of sorts – just the sort of thing his holy Order had been founded for. Unfortunately, whatever else it was, the Siege of Tangier turned out to be a complete disaster. Henry's generalship was lamentable. Not only was the city not taken, but his brother Ferdinand was. He spent the rest of his life an exile and a prisoner.

Ferdinand's death in 1443 triggered an intensive propaganda campaign on the part of the House of Aviz. While understandably playing down the role of Henry's incompetence in the prince's capture, this proclaimed his status as a near-saint; a martyr for his country and his church.

many people who said afterwards that it had been heard in Gibraltar.' The challenge the Christians faced was great, he noted:

Their enemies were many on the walls, and their strength was constantly increasing, and they defended the gate by casting before the Christians, from the height of the alls, stones and weapons ....

The rage of the Moors was such that at times, even without arms, they threw themselves upon the Christians; and their despair and their fury were so great that they did not surrender themselves, even if they found themselves alone before a multitude of enemies ...

Even so, within a matter of hours, Ceuta had been taken. The triumph was to turn out a slightly hollow one, however. It became clear relatively quickly that, unless it could take possession of Tangier too, Portugal couldn't hope to establish any real control over either Morocco or its trans-Sahara trade.

ORDER OF CHRIST

So strong has the Templar ideal proven that it has stirred excitement all the way down to the present day. It would have been surprising if it hadn't occasioned interest in its own time. Within a few years of the Templars' suppression, a new Order of Christ had been inaugurated by King Denis I of Portugal (1261–1325; reigned 1279–1325), based at the old headquarters of the Templars at Tomar, in Santarém. He persuaded Pope John XXII (1244–1334; reigned 1316–34) not only to give the new Order his official blessing but to license its possession of what had been Templar properties in Portugal.

A formidably fortified castle-cum-monastic complex, Tomar's Convent of Christ had been built in stages over the course of the twelfth century, during which time (in 1190) it had also seen off a major Moorish siege. Its imposing church, in keeping with the Templar tradition, was originally Romanesque in style and round in plan, like Jerusalem's Dome of the Rock. The construction of a rectangular nave around the old rotunda in the style of the fifteenth century added to the overall magnificence of the building, even if some of the old austerity of atmosphere was lost. The Convent complex also housed a palatial Grand Master's residence.

A short way across town is the thirteenth-century Church of Santa María do Olival (Our Lady of the Olive Grove), where over 20 Templar grand masters were lain to rest. In the Age of Discovery, however, this became the 'mother church' for Christians in Portugal's expanding empire in Africa, Asia and the New World. All in all a beautiful and fascinating medieval city, Tomar has become a shrine for twenty-first century Templar

Below: Vasco da Gama, the cross around his neck his constant guide.

THE CROSS AND THE CARAVEL

THE ORDER OF CHRIST was to be an important driver in Portugal's programme of colonial expansion – or, as this has also been known, the 'Age of Discovery'. As its Grand Master from 1417, Prince Henry the Navigator was told by King Duarte I that the Order could claim sovereignty in newly conquered territories – and, by Afonso V (1432–81; reigned 1438–81), that they could keep five per cent of the profits from any resulting trade. It was said to have been under the Order's aegis that a School of Navigation was set up at Sagres, at which a new generation of seafarers could be trained.

Vasco da Gama (c. 1460–1524) was in his later life to become a member of the Order of Christ. His voyage round the Cape of Good Hope to India predates that time. It can nevertheless be seen as showing his participation in a wider spiritual effort – even, indeed, as a sort of indirect crusade. Historian Nigel Cliff has put this case most strongly: The 'Age of Discovery' as a whole, in his analysis, wasn't just a competition between individual navigators, a space-race between the European powers of the fifteenth century or, for that matter, a straightforward imperialist adventure. Instead, the spirit of exploration emerged out of a continuing (but continuously modulating) geopolitical rivalry with the world of Islam: the riches of the Indies were to fund the crusade to end all crusades. With his attempt to find a Silk Road of the Sea, Cliff suggests, it was Vasco da Gama who engaged most directly with the Muslim foe, undertaking what were as much military expeditions as voyages of discovery.

tourists. What they come for isn't entirely clear; what they actually find still less so, but the sense that the Templars were in possession of strange 'secrets' seems irrepressible, now as then.

MAMLUK MENACE

Back in the Aegean, meanwhile, pressure on the Knights Hospitaller had only been growing. Rhodes seemed a long, long way from Christendom. In 1444, the Knights had held out against a major Muslim siege, this one mounted by a Mamluk invasion force from Egypt. The attackers had arrived in strength, on a fleet of 85 ships. They had stopped off to take the Hospitaller-held island of Kastellorizo before (on 10 August) landing on Rhodes' northwest coast a few miles from the capital.

The main invasion force headed straight for the city's western walls, focusing on what was generally regarded as their weak point, the St Anthony Gate. At the same time, moving southward, a second Mamluk party looped round to come at the Hospitallers' stronghold from the east. As they approached, they passed the harbour, sinking ships and burning buildings as they went.

Above: The St Anthony Gate at Rhodes, rebuilt on a massive scale, was now a mighty fortress in its own right.

The momentum was with the Mamluks, till an audacious sortie by French and Catalan knights from the safety of their stronghold caught the attackers off-guard and caused them many casualties. A second sortie, by Catalan knights, through the St Anthony Gate a few days later, dealt a definitive blow to Mamluk morale. In mid-September – so little more than a month after their arrival – the invaders withdrew in unseemly haste.

TURKISH TRAUMA

The Mamluks had come too close to victory for comfort, as far as the Hospitallers were concerned. In 1480, the Turks were to leave them traumatized. God's intervention had saved them – and emphatically underlined for them the rightness of their cause –

but they couldn't help pondering how things might have gone without his aid.

There was of course trauma for the Turks as well. To have come so close to taking the city and then to have failed was a crushing disappointment. Even if there's no real evidence they saw their defeat as owing anything to divine intervention, they didn't take the humiliation very well.

This is hardly surprising. After holding out against several centuries of Turkish attacks, the Byzantine capital, Constantinople, had in 1453 been taken by Sultan Mehmed II, 'the Conqueror'

Below: The saint won't worship pagan gods (foreground); is slaughtered (background); and borne aloft by angels in El Greco's *The Martyrdom of St Maurice.*

ST MAURICE'S MEN

COUNT AMADEO OF SAVOY (1383–1451) was not just a noble but (from 1439 to 1449) Felix V – one of a series of 'antipopes' set up in opposition to the ecclesiastical rule of Rome. If his papacy was contested, however, his personal piety wasn't. Nor was his good faith in founding the Order of St Maurice, in 1434. A military order from the start, it was named after St Maurice, who in 285 had led the so-called Theban Legion in their mass-conversion. These 6600 Roman soldiers were said to have embraced the faith of Christ together, and to have paid the price together, the following year, when all were martyred. St Maurice, widely venerated throughout the Alpine region, was believed to have been a cavalryman, so the obvious patron for a troop of mounted knights.

Like the other orders, that of St Maurice acquired important holdings in land and wealth – and, consequently, political influence – in Savoy. Of actual battle honours, rather less is known. The Order does appear to have owned and crewed a couple of galleys, which are said to have sailed with those of the Knights Hospitaller, but details of any such service remain scant.

(1432–81; reigned 1444–6 and 1451–81). As Istanbul, it had become the centre of a new and powerful Muslim state. The 'Ottoman Empire' took its name from its ruling dynasty's founder, the fourteenth-century Central Asian warlord Osman.

Above: Mehmed II leads his troops towards Constantinople, 1453.

Mehmed hadn't come – and conquered – this far to see his forces turned back by a bunch of monks. Like the other great Ottoman leaders, he was accustomed to leading his forces from the front, but had been too committed in southeastern Europe to be in Rhodes. This was still the case, but he remained resolved, immediately determining to send a still more formidable expedition against the island.

Within a year, however, he had died, after a sudden illness: there were rumours of a poisoning plot – and certainly much rejoicing across Christendom. Given the succession struggle that ensued, between Bayezid II (1447–1512; reigned 1481–1512) and his brother would-be Sultan Cem (1459–95), the Knights were actually in for an unexpectedly easy time.

RIGHT-HAND MAN

In 1482, Cem, on the run from his brother's forces, landed in Rhodes and begged for sanctuary with the Knights. He sought

Right: Mehmed II
directs his officers in a
scene from the Siege of
Constantinople, 1453.

their protection while he canvassed western capitals for military support against Bayezid, whom he still hoped – with Christian help – to overthrow. Grand Master D'Aubusson, however, reached a secret agreement with the Sultan. As long as he was prepared to leave them in peace, the Knights Hospitaller would hold on to Cem and make sure he stayed out of trouble. In the nicest possible way, he'd be their prisoner.

So grateful was the Sultan to the Order that he sent them a precious relic of their patron saint: the right hand of John the Baptist; the hand he'd baptised their Saviour Jesus with. Their spiritual exhilaration aside, the Knights were overjoyed to find this sort of charm offensive replacing actual Ottoman attack.

DEFENCE IN DEPTH

STONE WALLS AND EARTHEN ramparts around the citadel itself were only one aspect of Rhodes' defences. The Hospitallers had a sophisticated early-warning system. Their presence in preceptories across the Dodecanese as a whole had allowed for the construction of a network of castles and watchtowers. There were, the historian Zsolt Hunyadi has shown, well over twenty such outposts on the island of Rhodes; nine on Kastellorizo; eight on Kos; five on Kalymnos and several more on Symi, Alimnia and Leros. Signals sent with smoke, during daylight hours, and fire at night enabled messages to be passed from island to island. It's believed to have been for this reason that the Mamluks had stopped to take Kastellorizo before their attack on Rhodes of 1444.

By contrast, the failure of the Turks to spot the significance of the outpost on Alimnia as they gathered to mount their assault in 1480 is thought to have stood the Knights Hospitaller in good stead. It's known, Hunyadi tells us, that the Turks had been testing out the system regularly from as early as 1470. They were to continue doing so into the sixteenth century.

Below: A ruined Hospitaller castle on the island of Kos – one of many across the Dodecanese.

No one was under any illusion that the Hospitallers had bought themselves security for the longer term, however. Once Cem was dead, their bargaining position would be lost. There was, of course, a deeper question: was an accommodation of this kind with a warlike Muslim ruler really the aim towards which an order like theirs ought to be striving? In the absence of any reassuring answer, that question mostly went unasked. The fact was, the Knights Hospitaller were on the ropes. D'Aubusson was too shrewd to imagine that miracles could make

Right: Pierre d'Aubusson meets the Turkish runaway Cem aboard his ship, in Rhodes Harbour, 1482.

a satisfactory substitute for a defensive strategy. He set about strengthening Rhodes' fortifications. Over the following few decades, they were all to be substantially rebuilt – made longer, higher and better-proofed against cannon fire. The last of these aims – paradoxically, perhaps – was achieved by giving the walls soft centres. Behind an outer face of masonry, a core of earth absorbed the shock of any impact.

The city's defences were also doubled up, a higher, inner wall allowing fire to be maintained on an attacking force if the first, outer wall should be successfully scaled or breached. The Gate of St George was so radically reconceived – reconstructed on a pentagonal plan to facilitate defensive fire – that it amounted to a major fortress in its own right. The same might be said of St John's Gate, and of the Tower of St Nicholas, at the outer entrance to Rhodes' harbour.

MONUMENT TO MYTH

ROSSLYN CHAPEL, Midlothian, Scotland, was built in the middle of the fifteenth century – so a century and a half after the suppression of the Knights Templar. As we've seen, though, if the Order had an institutional afterlife in organizations like Portugal's Order of Christ, its mythic half-life has endured into the present day.

Much more recent interest has been stirred by Dan Brown's novel, *The Da Vinci Code* (2003) – which, of course, had a cameo role for Rosslyn. We've seen already that the secrecy that was a source of the military orders' strength was also to license the sort of speculation that would eventually bring them down. That same sense of mystery has attended on their histories ever since.

As for Rosslyn and its 'Templar Connection', the scholarship counsels scepticism at the very least. Not that more forthright debunkings don't abound. The historical facts – to agnostic modern eyes every bit as strange as any fiction – suggest that the chapel was built by the local Sinclair family as a burial place, and also as a sort of 'prayer factory', in which masses might be offered for the departed in a continuous cycle. This, it was hoped, would expedite the salvation of Sinclair souls stuck in Purgatory. This divine work was originally intended to go on in perpetuity, but was cut short by the Scottish Reformation of 1560.

7

A LONG RETREAT

The sixteenth century saw a steep decline in the fortunes of the military orders. Were they really going to find a role in the modern world?

ANOTHER CENTURY, another Siege of Rhodes. Again, the Ottoman Turks were the attackers. Sultan Suleiman I (1494–1566; reigned 1520–66) was great-grandson of the Mehmed II whose forces had come so close to taking the island back in 1480.

Even then, the Hospitallers had been very much the underdogs. Whether we see their deliverance as divinely ordained or as a simple stroke of immense good luck, it had been very much against the run of strategic play. And things were quite different now. With Suleiman the Magnificent's reign, a great empire was approaching its height. He'd taken Belgrade just the year before, laying open the way into central Europe, but was now consolidating his position closer to home.

Opposite: Galleys and ground troops mass in attack, while defenders hold out heroically in an exciting scene from the Siege of Rhodes in 1480.

The Knights Hospitaller's presence in Rhodes had been irksome to the Turks from the very first – for the same reasons that the Order had chosen it to be their base. Though nominally a 'Greek' island, it was almost within touching distance of Anatolia, the Turkish mainland; from there large areas of the Mediterranean could be controlled.

Below: Philippe de Villiers de l'Isle Adam carries a plan for some of the fortification work he presided over on Rhodes.

OVERWHELMING FORCE

The Hospitallers' Grand Master, Philippe de Villiers de l'Isle-Adam (1464–1534; in office 1524–34), had kept up the work of fortification that Pierre d'Aubusson had started. Just a year after the siege, in 1481, a setback had been suffered when a powerful earthquake rocked the island. But the Knights had set to and repaired the damage and carried on with their reinforcement work. Now, it would be fair to say that Rhodes' constructed defences were formidable by any normal standards. So too was its garrison: with almost 7000 men (including some 700 Knights Hospitaller), it was as large as such a stronghold could comfortably hold.

But the forces Suleiman could marshal made an Ottoman attack an extraordinary threat. In June 1522, he sent 400 vessels with several thousand marines under the command of his vizier Çoban Mustafa Pasha (?–1529). They softened up the island's defences over several days. Though excluded from the harbour by a chainlink boom, they still kept up a barrage of fire from the seaward side, destroying shipping and bombarding port installations and warehouses. Scores of land-based cannon kept up a constant fire from their positions on higher ground, tearing a ragged hole in the fabric of the city.

By the time Suleiman himself arrived with 100,000 men, at the beginning of July, Rhodes had already taken a severe battering. And this had been just a taster. In the weeks that followed, Turkish engineers tunnelled beneath important positions in hopes of undermining them and blew up barrels of gunpowder under vulnerable points along the city walls. They had some success, bringing sections of masonry crashing, leaving breaches into which their infantrymen could quickly rush – but they only found themselves under fire from Christian defenders on the inner walls.

LAST STAND

Such was the Hospitallers' resilience and courage that Rhodes remained untaken by late September. Mustafa Pasha tried to force the issue with one last all-out attack. This too was valiantly repulsed, and Mustafa was relieved of his duties by an angry Suleiman, who was only with difficulty dissuaded from having his general executed.

But his replacement, Ahmed Pasha (?–1524) didn't fare much better. Like Mustafa, he made modest gains but couldn't make the final breakthrough. He too made a final throw, in late November; and he too failed.

Both sides by now were running out of fight, but neither had the strength to capitalize on the other's weakness. The Christians had lost 5000 men – the greater part of their strength – and those who had survived were starving. Despite large losses of their own, the Turks were on the face of it still far stronger – but disease was spreading within their ranks, and morale collapsing. Suleiman decided he was willing to come to terms.

Above: Suleiman I, his magnificence upstaged by his headgear in this portrait, supposedly by Titian, c. 1530.

MOVING ON

But the sultan still felt he was in a strong position. Certainly sufficiently so to react with anger when (in his view) quibbling objections were made to his proffered truce. He ordered his forces to resume their attack till the Christians surrendered. On 22 December they finally did, and despite the trouble they had put him to through so many bitter weeks and months, found Suleiman in admirably magnanimous mood.

He had wanted the Hospitallers out of Rhodes – just as his forebears had for several generations now – but didn't appear to feel any deeper vindictiveness. As long as they left (he gave them twelve days to organize their departure and get clear), they could go unmolested, as far as the sultan was concerned. They could take fifty ships along with their armour and their weapons – and their religious treasures (vestments, bibles, missals, chalices, monstrances, crucifixes and other items). The Christians they left behind would be respected; their homes and churches left intact; their rights and their religious traditions tolerated.

It didn't work out quite like that. Although the Knights themselves were indeed allowed to leave in peace, their departure was the signal for a spree of violence and pillage.

The Hospitallers, however, made it safely as far as Crete, whence they moved on quickly to find sanctuary in Sicily. There they stayed while de Villiers de l'Isle-Adam scouted about for more settled quarters. In 1530, the Holy Roman Emperor, Charles V (1500–58; reigned 1518–58), gave them the island of Malta as a base, along with its offshore islets of Gozo and Comino.

REJECTING ROME

In September 1522, even as Suleiman's troops had the Hospitallers under siege in Rhodes, a very different danger was appearing in the West. On the face of it, an improbable one for Christians to fear, given that it was an edition of the New Testament. This one, though, had been translated into German by Martin Luther (1483–1546).

A priest and a professor at the University of Wittenberg, Luther had already made the wrong kind of name for himself in Rome. He had been open and excoriating in his criticism of Church corruption – most egregiously the offering of indulgences (essentially, 'time off' the sufferings of Purgatory) for sale.

His argument for translating the Gospels – that the faithful should be able to read them for themselves – seems unexceptionable, even to good Catholics, today. At the time, though, the Church condemned his work: the uneducated would be led astray, it said, if they weren't guided in their interpretations of God's message by its priests. It was for their

Above: Philippe de Villiers de l'Isle Adam negotiates the Hospitallers' surrender with Suleiman I, bringing a brutal five-month siege to a welcome end.

Above: Martin Luther's German New Testament (here we see the start of St Matthew's Gospel) was influential in bringing on the Reformation.

protection that his Word should remain in Latin. We've already seen that a new middle class was beginning to emerge in Germany – the same was happening across northern Europe as a whole. To an increasing number of people – typically literate, and schooled too in self-reliance – the Church's vaunted concern seemed condescending.

Catholicism had never had the right to claim proprietorship over the 'keys of heaven', a new type of 'Protestant' Christian was arguing. The individual should have his or her own relationship with God. The Pope and his priests might be admirable men (not that recent history appeared to confirm this), but their pronouncements had no special authority. What mattered was the divine Word, as revealed in the scriptures, which it was the duty of every man and woman to read. Protestants, it could be argued, took more moral responsibility for themselves – they saw no prospect of 'buying' indulgence with money, or by pattering mechanically through sets of prayers.

REFORMATION AND REACTION

The advent of Protestantism meant a paradigm shift for a Catholic Europe that had for centuries defined itself against the threat from Islam. There had always been odd heresies, but this was a major movement which represented a new and sinister 'enemy within'. Protestants didn't just reject the authority of the Church, but to some extent that of the state as well. They looked to their own individual consciences as arbiters of what was right and wrong – a recipe for anarchy, Europe's Catholic establishment feared.

Their concerns were not unjustified. If Protestantism as a religious movement mainly influenced the middle class, in the towns and cities, its rhetoric of liberation trickled down. Across the countryside, the common people, for many decades mired in helpless resentment of their local landowners, found the inspiration that they needed to rise up. A squirearchy of local gentry availed themselves of the unrest to stage their own revolts, against their aristocratic overlords.

THE TABLES TURNED

The so-called German Peasants' War of 1524–5 was an early test
for the Teutonic Knights. Though not explicitly a religious conflict,
it quickly came to shape itself along those lines – especially in areas
where perceived oppressors were associated with the Church.
They could hardly be more closely associated than the Teutonic
Knights, of course, and the Order became a target as a result.
This was in large part through their own fault: we've already seen
that they were exacting – and even rapacious – landlords.

In many places, plunder-hungry peasants were directed by
rebel ringleaders to attack the Teutonic Knights' preceptories
rather than the properties of local gentry – or even other orders'
religious houses. In Bozen (now Bolzano, in the Italian Tirol),
rebel captain Michael Gaismayr (c. 1490–1532), made the local
headquarters of the Teutonic Knights his first call: the contents
of its treasury created the war-chest for his whole campaign.

Groups who had little else in common rose up in the course
of the German Peasants' War. One thing that did unite them
was their hatred of the Teutonic Knights. At Heilbronn, Baden-
Württemberg, the city council, along with a motley crew of

Left: Even by the bloody
standards of early-modern
Europe, the German
Peasants' War was
particularly unpleasant.

craftsmen and unskilled labourers allied with angry peasants in from the countryside against them.

Having sacked the Order's headquarters, the rebels staged a celebratory banquet in the refectory: the surviving Knights were forced to stand in attendance, their hats in their hands, and serve their 'guests'. They were the lords, they laughed, and the Knights the servants. While some broke into the treasury, emptying it of silver, others contented themselves with gifts in kind, loading up with everything from wine and furniture to food. Women cut up sacred vestments to make clothes for themselves and their children.

Like many popular uprisings, the episode took on a 'carnivalesque' character – and not just because (for some, at least) it was the most terrific fun. True carnival, it's been observed, rejoices in up-ending conventional hierarchies, humbling the 'high' and exalting what's been seen as 'low'.

Below: The new religion co-opts the authority of the old in this portrayal of Albert of Brandenburg as 'Church Father' St Jerome (347–420).

ALBERT'S APOSTASY

Perhaps the ultimate ignominy for the Teutonic Order came in 1525 with the defection of its Grand Master, Albert of Brandenburg (1490–1568; in office 1510–25). He actually converted to Protestantism – personally persuaded into this course by Martin Luther.

As Catholic critics weren't slow to point out, he had inducements. One was the right to marry, which was key to Lutheranism's vision for the clergy – another way of weakening the hold of Rome. Albert lost no time in exercising this, with Dorothea of Denmark (1504–47), whom he wed in 1526. The other – again at Luther's suggestion – was that he got to make the Teutonic Order's state into his own personal duchy.

Personally advantageous it may have been, but this was in many ways an awkward

APOSTATE ORDER

ONE BRANCH OF THE Teutonic Order, the Bailiwick of Utrecht, in the Netherlands, survived well into the seventeenth century. In 1637, with pressure mounting on Catholic institutions in what was now the adamantly Protestant Dutch Republic, its senior officials agreed to embrace the reformed religion in return for being allowed to keep their order. Though briefly suppressed in the 1800s, when the Netherlands were occupied by Napoleonic France, the Bailiwick remains in existence to this day. Now no more than a charity, it nevertheless still occupies the *Duitse Huis* headquarters which were first built for the Bailiwick in 1348.

settlement. For one thing, it depended on the blessing of King Sigismund I, 'the Old', of Poland (1467–1548; reigned 1506–48). A Protestant duchy, accordingly, owed its fealty to a Catholic kingdom. The 'Prussian Homage' seemed inherently unstable. Even so, it was to last till 1641.

As for the Teutonic Knights, they lingered on in Livonia (a territory which sprawled across what is now Lithuania, Latvia and parts of Estonia). There as elsewhere, though, their holdings were gradually to be broken up over the sixteenth and seventeenth centuries. They were secularized under the rule of aristocratic landlords.

Though much diminished, the Order continued to be a military force of sorts as late as the eighteenth century, albeit as an elite of commanders rather than as a company of battle-ready knights. They were only to be wound up formally as a military outfit in 1805. Even then, they would retain a religious and ceremonial role.

THE HOSPITALLERS WEREN'T EXACTLY ENTHUSED BY THE FIRST SIGHT OF THEIR NEW HOME.

MAROONED IN MALTA

They would be based here for more than 250 years and would come to be known as the 'Knights of Malta', but the Hospitallers weren't exactly enthused by their first sight of their new home. Though more than twice the size of Rhodes, its lack of tree cover

Above: The Hospitallers' Grand Master Jean Parisot de la Valette led a determined defence of Rhodes against the Turks in 1522.

gave it the appearance of a barren rock; it might have been milder than their former home, but it was a great deal drier too. Securing adequate supplies of drinking water was to be an ongoing problem for the Order here, and they were always to struggle for self-sufficiency in food.

Even so, it seems fair to say that their negative feelings resulted largely from the circumstances of their arrival, on 26 October 1530. There were only 400 of them left and they were almost completely bereft of funds. Fifty ships had ferried them from Rhodes to Crete, back in 1522. Three storm-beaten galleys – the *Santa Croce*, the *San Filippo* and the *San Giovanni* – could carry the entire Order now.

Malta's geographical shortcomings aside, the Knights felt compromised by being here. Not that they could have afforded (either economically or politically) to refuse the emperor's offer. Like his predecessor, Maximilian I (1459–1519; reigned 1508–19), Charles V was Holy Roman Emperor, but before his accession he had been the King of Spain. His reign gave what had been a Germanic, Austrian-centred empire a Spanish bias. Not in a nationalistic way – Charles himself had been born in Ghent, in what is now Belgium – but he'd increasingly identified himself with Spain. And it was from that part of his patrimony that Charles took Malta for the Knights – most of whom were French-descended, and wary of Spanish power.

A LONG RETREAT 201

THE MALTESE FALCON

CHARLES V's mother, Queen Joanna of Castile (1479–1555), has gone down in history as 'Joanna the Mad', but her son had his own eccentricities, it seems. How else to account for the rent he set the Hospitallers for their Maltese tenancy: the gift of a bird, to be handed over every year? The Order, he said, could occupy the island in perpetuity, on condition that annually, on All Saints' Day (1 November), they made 'the sole payment of a falcon' to the emperor or his viceroy.

Above: A falcon figure tops a Hospitaller's helmet which in turn adorns a Maltese column. For centuries, the bird has been an island emblem.

PRESENT DANGER

The emperor hadn't given them this new base out of the kindness of his heart. The Knights Hospitaller had a job to do in Malta. The Crusades might be long gone, but a state of low-intensity warfare still existed between the Ottoman Empire and Christian Europe. As the sixteenth century went on, the fighting would increasingly be contracted out to the Barbary Pirates on the Muslim side. At first, while the conflict seldom rose above the level of small-scale skirmishing, it was directed and conducted by the sultan's own officers and ships. (Even then, though, the hierarchy wasn't quite as rigid or the loyalties as clear-cut as we might imagine. Dragut Reis (1485–1565), who gloried in the honorific 'the Drawn Sword of Islam', was one of many who occupied the wide grey area between Ottoman official and Corsair.)

By experience and by training, the Knights Hospitaller were well-equipped to take on the Ottomans on their own terms. Quite frankly, they badly needed the booty too. Although both sides will have seen themselves as benevolently 'policing' the Mediterranean, they did so in large part by harassing and hijacking each other's shipping. And, of course, in what were at this time much the busiest waters in the world, vast profits were there waiting to be made. In addition to cargo goods, both sides took hostages, who could either be held to ransom or simply sold as slaves.

Overall, the Order flourished. It didn't have everything its own way, though. Inevitably, its vessels sometimes came off worse. Malta, moreover, was vulnerable to blockade, its limited agricultural production an endless problem: shortages of grain caused several famines. There were other pressures too: the Order's European holdings were in many cases being confiscated in the post-Reformation religious conflict that now had mainland Europe in its grip.

Below: Charles of Anjou looks out from his flagship off Messina during the War of the Sicilian Vespers.

AN EMBATTLED ISLAND

A BYZANTINE POSSESSION FROM the first half of the sixth century, Malta was seized by Arab attackers from North Africa in 870. Even as wars of conquest go, this proved a particularly unpleasant occupation: the islanders' brave resistance brought out the worst in the invaders.

Over the next few centuries, then, Malta was only scantly populated. Numbers grew after it was retaken by the West. More specifically by the Normans who, having first arrived on the island in 1091, made it an outpost of their Kingdom of Sicily from the twelfth century.

Sicily had carried on casting a shadow over Maltese affairs: never more so than in the War of the Sicilian Vespers. A

longstanding tussle for power between popes and emperors had turned toxic when Pope Urban IV (c. 1195–1264; reigned 1261–4) tried to do down the Holy Roman Empire's ruling house of Hohenstaufen by conferring the Sicilian throne on Charles I of Anjou (c. 1226–85; reigned Sicily 1266–85).

The fighting that followed this imposition came to a head in a popular uprising after evening service ('Vespers') in Palermo's Church of the Holy Spirit on Easter Monday, 1282. Insurrection became all-out war, fought in Sicily, mainland Italy and Spain, but the Angevin (pro-Anjou) cause suffered a fatal setback at sea, in Valletta's Grand Harbour, at the Battle of Malta, in 1283.

BESIEGED AGAIN

In retrospect, the Great Siege of Malta (1565) seems like one last, heroic fling for the Hospitallers. They saw off their old adversary, Suleiman I. Forty years before, he'd been happy enough to have them out of Rhodes. It was a tribute of sorts to the effectiveness of their operations out of Malta that the sultan now determined to destroy them once and for all.

Most evidently meaning business, his force descended on the island at dawn on 18 May, with 250 ships and up to 40,000 fighting men – against 500 Knights

Above: A map shows the deployment of forces around Malta at the time of the Great Siege (1565).

Hospitaller, and 3500 islanders and mercenaries. The defenders fought back ferociously under the leadership of the Hospitallers' Grand Master Jean Parisot de la Valette (1495–1568; in office 1557–68). A veteran of the Siege of Rhodes, now four decades older, wiser and more resolute, he was ready to do anything but give way now.

The Turks kept up a continuous onslaught against all the main fortresses protecting the Grand Harbour: St Elmo's, St Michael's and St Angelo's. The light from the flares and cannon-, mortar- and musket-fire made the night sky shine 'as bright as day', one witness said. Iron hoops well wrapped in flax and cotton were dipped in brandy and saltpetre and set ablaze by the Knights inside. Thrown from the battlements, they enveloped unfortunate attackers up to three at a time.

The Turks were determined – no quarter given. That was only to be expected, maybe, but they indulged in some deeply dubious 'psy-ops' too. Decapitating some of the Knights they killed, they attached their headless bodies to crosses and set them floating in the harbour in a grotesquely savage swipe at their Christian beliefs.

Not that De la Valette was in any mood to turn the other cheek. He used the severed heads of Turkish prisoners as

Right: Dragut dies dramatically in this scene from the Great Siege, imagined in 1867 by the Maltese painter Giuseppe Cali.

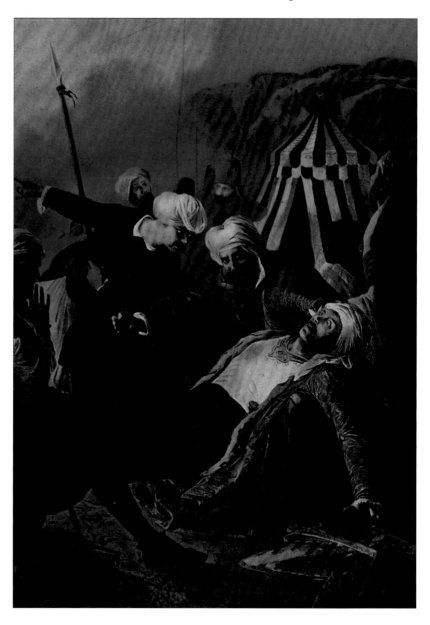

cannonballs, firing them back into their own lines, causing
consternation wherever they fell.

Dragut Reis, who came with fifteen ships and over a thousand
men, landed just to the north, at Marsamxett Harbour. He was
killed in fierce fighting on its northern shores, at what's now
known as Dragut Point. Suleiman's main force fared better:
St Elmo's Fort fell at the end of June, though the attack had cost
them dearly in casualties. An advance overland from the south
across the Senglea Peninsula allowed the Ottoman artillery to
line up above the Grand Harbour, subjecting it to what historians
have suggested may well have been the greatest bombardment the
world had at that time seen.

Weeks went by and successive Turkish attacks made real
encroachments on the Knights' positions without quite
managing to achieve that vital breakthrough. Forts St Michael
and St Angelo were badly battered but still held out. When the
Spanish nobleman Don García de Osorio, Marquis de Villafranca
(1514–77) arrived on 7 September with 8000 fresh fighting men,
this *Gran Soccorso* ('Great Rescue') was enough to demoralize
the weary Turks. Four days later, they weighed anchor and
sailed away.

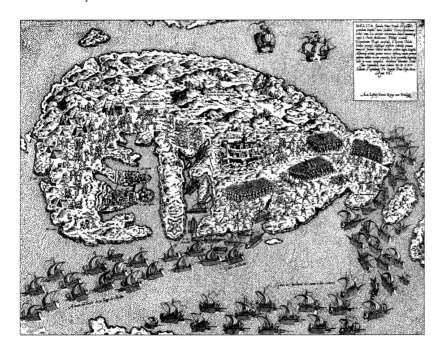

Left: Newly landed
from their fleet, Spanish
troops bring the
besieged Hospitallers
their *Gran Soccorso*
(7 September 1565).

CRUEL CORSAIRS

THE NOTORIOUS BARBARY PIRATES or corsairs – so called because they operated out of ports along North Africa's 'Barbary' (or Berber) Coast – were what later history would call 'privateers'. Essentially autonomous, out for themselves and independent of any real authority, they were nevertheless licensed to carry out their depredations by the sultan. Any irritation to the western powers was seen as furthering his wider cause. There were privateers on the European side as well (the Knights Hospitaller themselves can be seen as having had an analogous role), but their activities obviously escaped the criticism of the Christian chroniclers.

Not that the Barbary Pirates were by any means innocent. They stopped shipping at sea and raided coastal settlements throughout the Mediterranean. And, on occasion, well beyond: attacks were recorded as far afield as England's Bristol Channel and the West of Ireland. Whole communities were enslaved – more than a million, perhaps, in all – by the corsairs. They were ruthless with those who resisted them: thousands were killed.

Though the height of their activities was to be reached in the second half of the seventeenth century, the Barbary Pirates weren't definitively shut down until the 1820s.

On 21 December 1522 – the day before their surrender at Rhodes had brought down the curtain on a couple of hundred years of history – a glimpse of better things to come had been caught in Nice. There a giant carrack, the *Sant'Anna*, had been launched. It could carry 500 soldiers, in addition to its 300 crew.

Astern of its square-rigged fore- and mainmasts was a lateen-rigged mizzen – and, further back still, another lateen-rigged 'bonaventure' mast. It needed all the sail power it could muster, for it was not just huge but hugely heavy. Its hull between the waterline was covered with lead plating – mainly, it seems, to maintain perfect watertightness; two of its six decks were similarly lead-plated. Its fifty cannon were supplemented by a range of firearm weaponry which could be moved about on its various decks; there were small guns fixed high up on its rigging too.

FORWARD-LOOKING AS IT WAS, THERE DIDN'T SEEM TO BE ANYTHING FOR IT TO LOOK FORWARD TO.

It was designed to deal with Ottoman galleys – over 20 at a time if necessary. A ram built into its strengthened bow allowed it to run down any unfortunate ship that blocked its path; its richly ornamented stern reared high above any enemy vessel, giving Hospitaller sharpshooters free fire across its decks. Inside this multi-storey tower aft, along with accommodation for the officers, was a palatial council room for the Grand Master and his staff. The *Sant'Anna* could carry enough rations for continuous six-month tours at sea; it had a bakery so fresh bread could be had daily. In addition, it boasted a blacksmith's shop, assorted specialist workshops and a big and sophisticated armoury.

MALTESE CROSS

When we consider the history of the Knights Hospitaller from the 1520s, however, the *Sant'Anna* is just about nowhere to be seen. While it was to figure in the lifting of the Siege of Coron (Koroni, off western Greece) in 1532, it was too slow to keep up with the galleys sent to attack the Tunisian fortress of La Goletta, three years later. Ultra-modern it may have been, but this extraordinary ship doesn't seem to have had what it took to participate in a naval war that had its own conventions and

Opposite: A Spanish galley does battle with Barbary Pirates, painted by Andries van Eertvelt in the early seventeenth century.

Right: Antonio Martelli,
Prior of Messina and
leading Knight Hospitaller
sports an impressive
Maltese Cross in this
portrait by Caravaggio.

its own tactical rules. In 1540 – only eighteen years old – it was
decommissioned. Forward-looking as it was, there didn't seem to
be anything for it to look forward to. Did the Knights of St John
of Malta – as they were now known – have a future?

It doesn't appear to have been till now that the Order adopted
the eight-pointed Maltese Cross – the points are said to represent
the eight Beatitudes. These were the blessed states praised by
Christ in the Sermon on the Mount (Matthew 5): 'Blessed are
the poor in spirit … Blessed are those who mourn… Blessed are
the meek …'

They could, however, also symbolize the eight obligations the
Knights held dearest: Truth; Faith; Repentance; Humility; Love
of Justice; Mercy; Sincerity and Courage under Persecution.
Or, it's been hazarded too, the eight regions or *langues* into
which the Hospitaller world was at that point divided.

Great deeds were still to be done, and glorious victories still to be won, however, as the seventeenth century wound towards its conclusion. At Lepanto, in 1670, a Christian 'Holy League' was to triumph over a Turkish fleet in an epic clash of Cross and Crescent, of Christian West and Islamic East.

The battle was unprecedented in its scale: 'the greatest event witnessed by ages past, present and to come,' in the view of the Spanish writer Miguel de Cervantes (1547–1616), who was there. So traumatizing a spectacle was it that for another survivor it had the effect of completely altering reality: 'as if men were extracted from their own bodies and transported to another world'.

The Knights Hospitaller did their bit, and no doubt served with the utmost credit – but of the 212 Christian ships which prevailed that day over 270-odd Turkish vessels, only three galleys were theirs. Commendable enough, no doubt, but strictly marginal to the main action: the Knights were going to have to find another role.

Below: Its scale, its ferocity, its noise and its sheer confusion made the Battle of Lepanto something altogether new in naval warfare.

8

THE STUFF OF LEGEND

Modernity has seen the military orders all but disappearing as forces of real influence but renewing themselves as a semi-mythical idea.

A FRESH false start for the Knights Hospitaller in the Americas didn't augur well. That a string of 'Lascaris Towers' dotted about the coast of Malta have been the most enduring memorial to Giovanni Paolo Lascaris (1560–1657; in office 1636–57) is all the comment we really need about his term of office as the Knights' Grand Master.

NEW WORLD, NEW FAILURE
It had all been going to be so different, though. For in the 1640s, availing himself of the colonial connections of one of his Order's high officials, Phillippe de Longvilliers de Poincy (1584–1660), Lascaris had set about building a new future for the Hospitallers in the New World.

In 1651, the Order purchased the Caribbean island of Saint-Christophe (St Kitts), along with its offshore islands Saint

Opposite: Its intention of re-creating Solomon's shrine may have been hopeless, but London's Temple Church still has a special dignity.

Martin (now Nevis), Saint Barthélémy (St Barts) and Saint Croix. The venture wasn't to be a great success – at least not for the Knights Hospitaller. De Poincy went rogue and ran the colonies in his own interest. The home he built himself, the Château de la Montaigne, St Kitts, was considered one of the wonders of the Americas in its day – a tropical Versailles built by imported European craftsmen and staffed by 100 servants. The surrounding estate was worked by over 300 slaves. Not until after De Poincy's death would the Order at last be able to assert its ownership of the extravagant estate he'd built himself.

Below: A series of Lascaris Towers like this once guarded Malta's coasts. Of the ten originally built, nine still survive.

Work conditions in the feudal era would not of course have stood up to modern scrutiny, but those who worked for De Poincy – and hence the Hospitallers – were chattel-slaves. Not that this would have occasioned adverse comment from outside the Order (there's no indication of any real uneasiness within it) at that time, but it does point up how far the Knights had travelled, not just geographically but ethically.

From our point of view, the Château de la Montaigne has the character of a ghastly caricature, grotesquely parodying the old preceptories on which the Hospitallers' material fortunes had once been built. What, we wonder, would King Baldwin IV have made of the earthquake that destroyed the great house – and left the estate essentially unworkable – in 1689? Either way, that, substantially, was that for the Hospitallers' great colonial venture. They quietly let go of their Caribbean holdings.

Those they had in Europe that had survived the Reformation were for the most part lost in the upheavals accompanying the French Revolution (1789) and the ensuing wars. In 1798, Napoleon (1769–1821), en route to Egypt with bigger conquests in mind, took Malta as a resupplying station for his ships. Although Pope Leo XIII (1810–1903; reigned 1878–1903) was to revive the Order (as 'The Sovereign Military Order of Malta') in 1879, it was strictly as a humanitarian charity.

OCCULT AURA

Quite a come-down, then – though the Pope's decision not to found an all-new organization does point to the glamour still attaching to the medieval military orders. They were names – if no more than that – to conjure with. And Leo had been among the last to see this: since as long ago as the 1740s, when the Knights Hospitaller had still existed – just about – their myth had been co-opted by enthusiasts of the occult.

Most famously by the Freemasons, who since 1737 can boast (if a secret order can be boasted) their own 'United Religious, Military and Masonic Orders of the Temple and of St John of Jerusalem, Palestine, Rhodes and Malta' – or, for short, 'Knights Templar'. The wider Freemason movement was of course promiscuous in plundering ancient lore – from that of Egypt to that of Zoroastrian Persia and the pagan Middle East – though at this time a great many Masons saw themselves as modern-minded freethinkers. In this case, the religious associations of the title meant a little more, since members professed themselves believing Christians.

Below: Eighteenth-century freemasons await the arrival of the Masters. Their ceremonies owed much to a mythologized version of Templar rites.

Every great religious tradition has its mystic dimension, and with the help of hindsight we can certainly see that, since medieval times, Christian orthodoxy had been attended by its wilder, stranger spiritual fringe. While some, like Julian of Norwich (c. 1342–c. 1416), St Teresa of Ávila (1515–82) and St John of the Cross (1542–91), had looked inward to find their way out of a world of earthbound reality, others had sought an esoteric wisdom in older traditions of the occult.

EVERY GREAT RELIGIOUS TRADITION HAS ITS MYSTIC DIMENSION.

THE TEMPLARS TRANSFORMED

The would-be science of alchemy is now remembered mainly for its efforts to turn base metal into gold, but devotees were actually to spread their intellectual net more widely. The interest in this area of such serious researchers as Robert Boyle (1627–91) and Isaac Newton (1642–1726) can hardly be seen as assuring its scientific respectability in the modern age. It's a valuable corrective, even so, to those self-consciously sceptical modern thinkers who'd dismiss such ideas, as held historically, as simply 'stupid'. If the alchemists never did succeed in turning lead into gold, they did collectively transmute the history of the Knights Templar into a thrillingly vibrant (if mostly bogus) mystic myth.

The web of justificatory pseudo-history with which the alchemists progressively enveloped their researches had a starring role for the Knights Templar in particular. Their (alleged) association with Solomon's Temple offered at least the semblance of a connection with the Judaeo-Christian tradition's deepest roots. That, unlike the Hospitallers, the long-abolished Templars didn't have any recent real-life history to impede the freest flights of speculation made them a particularly appealing focus for such 'research'.

From the Rosicrucians of the Renaissance all the way down to the Order of the Golden Dawn in the twentieth century, the Knights Templar were to find esoteric followers in the modern world. They were, of course, never really more than one among a miscellany of mystic 'props' that included items drawn from everywhere from early-modern European neo-Platonism to the Jewish Kabbalah and (Egyptian-originated) tarot cards.

THE KNIGHTS AND THE NOVEL

THE OCCULTIST VIEW OF the Knights Templar was of course to be dazzlingly articulated in *The Da Vinci Code*, a novel which made a feature of its breadth of mystic reference. Disdainful swipes at its prose apart, the most striking feature of its reception was perhaps that its admirers and detractors were so often thrilled or irritated by the same things. And that these were in their turn the exact same things which, as far as we can tell over a great many centuries, had exhilarated lovers or alienated despisers of the occult.

Untrammelled ingenuity in conception; twist after twist in narrative progression; conspiratorial convolution as default ... Dan Brown's fiction offered up a world in which nothing could ever be quite as it seemed – yet which revolved around a quasi-chivalric quest for a grail of truth. Definitively, unimpeachably, historically real yet at the same time mythically remote and essentially mysterious, the Knights Templar had an obvious part to play in such a book.

GERMAN VERSIONS

However wrong-headed they may have been, these mystic re-imaginings of the Templar ethos have at least acknowledged their truly 'Catholic' – and hence trans-national – appeal. But, nationalism of a more or less benign description being the mood of the moment in mid-nineteenth-century Europe, it was inevitable that some would see things differently. That national consciousness could take on a more sinister character was made more and more clear in the developing operatic *oeuvre* of Richard Wagner (1813–83). The Knights of the Grail in *Parzifal* (1882), his version of Wolfram von Eschenbach's great medieval romance, were widely seen as referencing the Knights Templar. But, it seemed, with something quintessentially German in their mystic strength.

The story of the Teutonic Knights was taken up in the twentieth century, when the Order was seen as emblematic of a

WAGNER'S *PARZIFAL* WAS WIDELY SEEN AS REFERENCING THE KNIGHTS TEMPLAR.

new and potent Germany. All the major European powers were seeking to build empires in Africa and Asia at this time, and Kaiser Wilhelm II (1859–1941; reigned 1888–1918), who in 1901 had promised his German subjects 'a place in the sun', liked to see himself as latter-day Knight of the Order. As the Knights had in their 'Northern Crusade', now the Kaiser's imperial army would cut a conquering swathe through Africa and the Far East.

The Nazis were drawn to the iconography of the Teutonic Knights for the same reasons. While they suppressed what was left of the actual order, seeing it (quite rightly) as loyal to the Catholic Church, they unabashedly appealed to its romance. The *Schutzstaffel* or SS was deliberately conceived as recalling the Order in its organization – and, of course, in the heroic role it was to play in building the new Nazi nation.

Others made the connection between the Teutonic Knights and Hitler's Germany, but didn't appear to admire it quite so much. In his film *Alexander Nevsky* (1938), the celebrated Soviet director Sergei Eisenstein (1898–1948) memorably evoked the knights' defeat at Lake Peipus, 1242.

Above: Parsifal's quest, as imagined by the German artist Ferdinand Leeke in 1912. Medieval myth had found a new lease of modern life.

CONTINUING CARE

Meanwhile, Pope Leo's 'Sovereign Military Order of Malta' carries on quietly with its work of providing medical assistance, in disaster situations or simply in poor countries, around the world. Although explicitly a Catholic order, it is committed to providing help to those who need it regardless of their ethnicity or faith. It has some 13,500 full members, but they can call on 40,000 trained doctors and nurses, and over twice that many volunteers.

Unlike the original Hospitallers, its knights (and dames) are neither ordained clergy nor professional soldiers, but lay men and women, honoured for their service to humanity and the Church. And it is an honour to have membership in the world's oldest chivalric order – far as its work may be removed from what it was in the days of the Crusades.

HOSPITALLERS STILL

Sᴛ Jᴏʜɴ's Gate in London's Clerkenwell district dates back to 1504. It was built by the Grand Prior of the Knights Hospitaller in England, Thomas Docwra (c. 1458–1527; in office 1502–57) as part of the Order's main headquarters in the country. Over subsequent centuries, while much of the foundation was cleared away, this gatehouse survived, becoming an important local landmark. In the 1870s, it was adapted to house the head office of a newly inaugurated 'Order of St John'. Though no longer a military order, it still held to Hospitaller principles with its work of supporting projects in emergency medicine and public health.

Above: St John's Gate endures as a memorial to the Knights Hospitaller in modern London.

An earlier attempt at founding such an order in the 1830s had met with hostility from the Catholic Church. Now, however, no one worried what Rome might feel. Alfred Lord Tennyson (1809–92) had rediscovered the Arthurian romances for a modern age and the vogue for medievalism had made its mark on everything from the architecture of Augustus Pugin (1812–52) to the Pre-Raphaelite art of Dante Gabriel Rossetti (1828–82), William Holman Hunt (1827–1910) and John Everett Millais (1829–96). The Middle Ages weren't just fashionable now: they felt as if they were the property of all. No one saw anything odd about the idea of a predominantly Anglican, but ecumenical, Order of St John.

Officially chartered by Queen Victoria (1819–1901; reigned 1837–91) in 1888, this new order has endured down to the present day. While still centred in the United Kingdom, it is active across the British Commonwealth – and in many other countries in Europe and worldwide. Its Sovereign Head is Queen Elizabeth II. To many, it is most familiar from the St John Ambulance Brigade whose volunteers offer first-aid support at public occasions and sporting events.

BIBLIOGRAPHY

Armstrong, Karen, *A History of Jerusalem: One City, Three Faiths* (London: HarperCollins, 1996).

Brown, Dan, *The Da Vinci Code* (New York: Doubleday, 2003).

Campbell, David, *Templar Knight vs Mamluk Warrior*, 1218–50 (London: Bloomsbury, 2015).

Cliff, Nigel, *The Last Crusade: The Epic Voyages of Vasco da Gama* (London: Atlantic, 2012).

Crowley, Roger, *Empires of the Sea: The Final Battle for the Mediterranean, 1521–80* (London: Faber, 2008).

__, *Conquerors: How Portugal Forged the First Global Empire* (London: Faber, 2015).

Eschenbach, Wolfram von (tr. Hatto, A.), *Parzival* (London: Penguin Classics, 1980).

Haag, Michael, *The Templars: History and Myth* (London: Profile, 2009).

__, *The Tragedy of the Templars and the Crusader States* (London: Profile, 2012).

Hunyadi, Zsolt, 'Early-Warning Systems and the Hospitallers in the Eastern Mediterranean', in Giannokopoulos, Georgios and Sakas, Damianas P. (eds), *Advances on Information Processing and Management*, Piraeus, Greece: Institute for the Dissemination of Arts and Science, 2011.

Langan, John, 'The Elements of St Augustine's Just War Theory', *Journal of Religious Ethics*, vol. 12, no. 1, Spring 1984, pp. 19–38.

Lord, Evelyn, *The Knights Templar in Britain* (Harlow: Longman, 2002).

Muscat, Joseph, 'Warships of the Order of St John', in *Proceedings of History Week*, Valletta: Malta Historical Society, 1994.

Napier, Gordon, *The Rise and Fall of the Knights Templar: The Order of the Temple, 1118–1314* (Staplehurst, Kent: Spellmount, 2003).

Nicholson, Helen, *The Knights Hospitaller* (Woodbridge, Suffolk: Boydell, 2001).

__, (ed.), *The Military Orders, Volume II: Welfare and Warfare* (London: Routledge, 1998).

Partner, Peter, *The Knights Templar and their Myth* (Rochester, VT: Destiny, 1990).

Peters, F.E. (ed.), *Jerusalem: The Holy City in the Eyes of Chroniclers, Visitors, Pilgrims and Prophets from the Days of Abraham to the Beginnings of Modern Times* (Princeton: Princeton University Press, 1985).

Riley-Smith, Jonathan, *The Oxford History of the Crusades* (Oxford: OUP, 2003).

Sebag-Montefiore, Simon, *Jerusalem: The Biography* (London: Weidenfeld & Nicolson, 2011).

Staunton, Michael, *The Historians of Angevin England* (Oxford: OUP, 2017).

Sumption, Jonathan, *The Albigensian Crusade* (London: Faber, 1998).

Théry, Julien, 'A Heresy of State: Philip the Fair, the Trial of the "Perfidious Templars," and the Ponticalization of the French Monarchy,' *Journal of Medieval Cultures*, Vol. 39, no. 2, 2013.

Throop, Susanna A., *Crusading as an Act of Vengeance, 1095–1216*, (Farnham, Ashgate: 2011).

Troyes, Chrétien de (tr. Carroll, Carleton and Kibler, William),

Tull, George F., *Traces of the Templars* (Rotherham: King's England Press, 2000).

Tyerman, Christian (ed.), *Chronicles of the First Crusade* (London: Penguin Classics, 2011).

INDEX

References to illustrations are
in *italics*

Acre 75, 105–7, 109, *109*, 130–1,
130
Ad providam 153, 154
Al-Adil I 124–6
Adramyttium, Battle of (1334) 162
Afonso I, King of Portugal 79, *79*
Afonso V, King of Portugal 182
Ahmed Pasha 193
Al-Aqsa Mosque 8, *9*, 63, *63*, 104
Albert of Brandenburg 198–9, *198*
Albigensian Crusade *122*, 123
alchemy 214
Aleppo, Syria 97
Alexander III, Pope 96
Alexander IV, Pope 75
Alexander Nevsky (film) 216
Alexandria, Egypt 165
Alexandrian Crusade (1365) 165
Alexius I 51
Alfonso VII, King 78
Aljiubarrota, Battle of (1385) 179
Amadeo of Savoy, Count 184
Amalric, King of Jerusalem 96, *96*
Amalric of Tyre 137
Americas 211–12
Amorgos, Battle of (1312) 158
Andrew II, King of Hungary 88,
124
Andronicus II, Emperor 138
Anglo-Saxon Chronicle 64, 66
Antioch, Syria 52, 54, 55, 56, 104
antipopes 184
apostolic succession 43
Aragón, Spain 78, 119
Araima 89
Armenia *164*
armour 70
arrests of the Templars 146–8, *147*
Arsuf 107–8, *108*
Arthur, King 29, 30, 31
as-Salih, Al Malik 127
Ascalon (Ashkelon) 8, 90, 92–4,
99, 102
Assailly, Gilbert d' 96
assassinations 89–90
Asturias 78, 79
Atlit, Israel 125
Aubusson, Pierre d' *166*, 168, *168*,
186, 188, *188*

Austria 105, 107
Avignon, France 142
Aydinids 158, 160, 162
Azurara, Gomes Eannes de 180–1

Bha ad-Din 13
Baibars 127
Bailiwick of Utrecht 199
Baldwin I, King of Jerusalem 26, 54
Baldwin II, King of Jerusalem *53*,
62, *62*, 66, 87
Baldwin III, King of Jerusalem 86,
87, *87*, 92, 93, *94*, 97
Baldwin IV, King of Jerusalem 7–14,
75, 87, 99–100, 173
Baltic Slavs 131–2
Banias Castle 97
banking 119–20, 121
banners 77
Baphomet 145
Barbary Pirates 206
Barres, Everard de 83, 85
Bayezid II 185–6
Beatriz of Portugal 177, 179
Beaufort Castle 128
Beaujeu, Guillaume de 130
Becket, Thomas 95
Belgium 118, 143
Benedict XI, Pope 142
Benedictine monks 36–41, 69
Benedictine Rule 38–9, 40
Béziers, France 123
Bible 16–17, 20
Bilbeis, Egypt 96
Blanquefort, Bertrand de 97
Bogusza 176
Boniface VIII, Pope 141–2, *142*, 143
Bouillon, Godfrey de 25, 51, 52, 57
Bozen 197
Brown, Dan 189, 215
Burchard III, Archbishop 151–2
Byzantines 44–5, 46, 47, 51, 83, 85,
138, 184–5

Calatrava la Vieja, Spain 78
Camelot 30
cannons 172, *172*
Canterbury Tales, The 27, 95
Caoursin, Guillaume 170
Caribbean 211–12
Castell de Castells, Spain 178
Castellum Bochee 59

Castile 78, *177*, 178
castles/properties
Knights Hospitaller 86, 88–9, *89*,
97, 109, 118–19, 136, *138*, 140,
140, 183, *183*, 189, 212, *212*,
217
Knights Templar 86, 88, 95, *95*,
109, *109*, *115*, 115–18, *117*,
125, 125, 128, *136*, *210*
see also monastic estates
Cathars 122–3
Celestine II, Pope 67
Celestine V, Pope 141
celibacy 42, 72, 73
Cem, Sultan 185–6, 188, *188*
Cervantes, Miguel de 29, 209
Ceuta, Morocco 179–81
Charles I of Anjou 202
Charles II of Anjou 141, 142
Charles V, Holy Roman Emperor
195, 200, 201
Charney, Geoffroi de 153–4, *153*
Chastel Blanc 129
chastity 73
Château de la Montaigne, St Kitts
212
Château Pèlerin, Israel *125*, 125
Chaucer, Geoffrey 27, 37, 95
Chinon Parchment 150, *151*
chivalry 28–31
Chrétien de Troyes 31, 113–14
Cistercian monks 69
Cîteaux, France 69
Civitate 45, 47
Clairvaux, France 69, *69*
Clement V, Pope 142, *142*, *144*,
148, 150–3, *152*, 155
Clement VI, Pope 162, *163*, 164
clerical celibacy 42
Cliff, Nigel 182
clothing 70, 72, *72*
Çoban Mustafa Pasha 192–3
Colonna family 141, 142, *142*
commandries 116
Conrad II, Emperor 42
Conrad III, King of Germany 82,
84, *84*, 90, 92
conspiracy theories 129
Constantine the Great 15, 19, 43–4
Constantinople 46, *120*, 122,
184–5, *185–6*
Corsairs 206

Coulommiers, France 117–18
Council of Clermont (1095) 47–8
Council of Troyes (1129) 66, 113
Covadonga, Battle of (722) 78
Crac des Chevaliers 59, 86, 88–9, 89, 129
Cressing Temple, Essex 115, 115
Crusade of Kings see Third Crusade
Crusader States 54, 55
Cyprus 135–7, 136, 157, 162

Da Vinci Code (Dan Brown) 189, 215
Damascus 7, 85
Damietta, Siege of (1217–18) 124, 124
Dandolo, Enrico 120
Dante 37, 74, 172
Danzig 176
Denis I, King of Portugal 148, 150, 181
Des Barres, Everard 83, 86
Des Roches, Peter 109
Docwra, Thomas 217
Dome of the Rock 63
Don Quixote 29
Donation of Constantine 43–4
Dorothea of Denmark 198
Dorylaeum, Turkey 84, 84
Dragut Reis 201, 204, 205
du Puy de Provence, Raymond 93, 93
Duarte I, King of Portugal 179, 182
Durbe, Battle of (1260) 132

East-West Schism 46
Edessa
   as Crusader State 54, 55, 56
   fall of 81, 91
   resistance from Muslims 97
education of knights 33, 35
Edward I, King of England 128, 143
Edward II, King of England 148, 150, 155
Egypt 96, 124, 127, 165
Eighth Crusade (1270) 128
Elaine of Corbenic 34
England
   and France 65, 143
   Knights Hospitaller 119, 217
   Knights of St Thomas 109
   Knights Templar 95, 115–16, 118, 210, 217, 217
   London 65, 95, 109, 116, 118, 210, 217, 217

Ninth Crusade 128
Order of St John 217
place names 117
properties in 95, 115–16, 118, 210, 217, 217
support for Templars 95, 148
Third Crusade 104, 106–7
Eschenbach, Wolfram von 31, 112, 112, 215
Eugene III, Pope 67, 81–2, 83, 83
Évora, Portugal 79
exploration 182

Famagusta, Cyprus 136
farms/farming 54, 115, 118, 178
Fatimids 91–4, 96
Felix V (antipope) 184
Fenham, Newcastle 119
Ferdinand, Infante 180
Ferdinand I of Portugal 177
Ferdinand IV of Castile 150, 155
Fernández Andeiro, Juan 179
feudalism 54–5
Fifth Crusade (1217–21) 123–6
First Crusade (1096–9) 8, 25, 49–54, 50–2
flags 77
forestry 119
Floyran, Esquin de 146
Fourth Crusade (1202–4) 120, 120
France
   Cathars 122–3
   Eighth Crusade 128
   and England 65, 143
   First Crusade 51–2
   funding of Templars 64, 83
   monasteries 69
   Moors 60, 77
   papacy moves to 142
   Philip IV (Philip the Fair) 141–3, 143, 144–9, 149, 151–2, 154, 155
   properties in 117–18
   Second Crusade 82–5
   Seventh Crusade 127
   Third Crusade 104, 106–7
Frederick I Barbarossa, Emperor 104–5
Frederick II, Emperor 124, 126
Freemasons 213, 213
Fulcher of Chartres 47–8, 53
Fulk, King of Jerusalem 59, 75, 87
funding of knights 64–7, 83, 88, 90, 95, 114–15, 119–20, 121

Gaismayr, Michael 197
Galicia 78, 179
Galilee, Principality of 56
galleys 159, 159
Genoa 120, 158
Geoffrey of Monmouth 30
Germany
   Fifth Crusade 124
   Peasants War 197–8, 197
   Second Crusade 82, 84
   Third Crusade 105
   tribunals of Templar 152
   see also Teutonic Knights
God, intervention of 13–15
Golden Bull of Rieti 132
Grand Master's Palace, Rhodes 138, 140, 140
Great Mosque of Córdoba 77
Gregory IX, Pope 132
Guillaume of Chartres 124
Guinevere, Queen 29, 31, 32
Guy, King of Jerusalem 105

Haakon Paulsson, Earl 22
Hagia Sophia 46
Al-Hakim bi-Amr Allah 91, 91
Halston, Shropshire 118
Hashashin 89–90, 90
Heilbronn, Germany 197–8
Henriques, Pedro 79
Henry II, King of England 65, 95
Henry II, King of Jerusalem 136–7
Henry III 42
Henry the Navigator 179, 179, 180, 182
heresy 123
Hisham I 77
Historia Regum Britanniae 30
Holy Grail 30–1, 111–12
Honorius II, Pope 66, 114
Horns of Hama, Battle of (1175) 98
Horns of Hattin, Battle of (1187) 100–2, 100, 101
Horsleydown, London 118
Hospital of St John of Jerusalem 56–8, 56
hospitals 56–8, 56
Hot, Arnold 123
Hungary 124
Hunyadi, Zsolt 187

Ice, Battle of the (1242) 133, 133
imprisonment 154
In Praise of the New Knighthood 66
Inferno (Dante) 37

initiation ceremony *71*, 73–5
Innocent II, Pope 67, *67*, 83, 123
Ismat ud-Din Khatun 98

Jadwiga of Poland, Princess 173, *173*
Jagiellonian Dynasty 173–6
James II of Aragon 146, 150
Jerusalem *126*
  captured by Turks 126–7
  Christian prisoners *103*
  civil war 87
  as Crusader State 54, *55*, 56
  and Fatimids 96
  Fifth Crusade 123–6
  First Crusade 52–3, 54
  loss of credibility 85–6
  in Muslim hands 48–9, *103*, 104, 108, 126–7
  panic of Christians 102
  return to Christians 126
  Second Crusade 85–6
  Sixth Crusade 126
  St John's hospital 56–8, *56*, 104
  and Saladin 7–10, *103*, 104
Jews 51, 143, 149
João I, King of Portugal 177, *177*, 179
Jogalio of Lithuania 173–5, *173*
John XXII, Pope 181
Juan I of Castile 177, 179
Juan II 178
Jungingen, Ulrich von 175
Just War 21

al-Kamil, Sultan 126
Kastellorizo 183, 187
Kerullarios, Michael 46
Khwarezmiyya 126
Kilmainham, Dublin 119
King Arthur 34, 37
knighthoods 33, 35–6, *36*
Knights Hospitaller
  at Acre 130–1
  Alexandrian Crusade 165
  in the Americas 211–12
  and Armenia *164*
  at Ascalon (Ashkelon) 93
  attacks on ships 158, 160–3, *160–1*
  besieged at Banias 97
  at Bilbeis, Egypt 96–7
  castles/properties 86, 88–9, *89*, 97, 109, 118–19, *136*, 138, 140, *140*, 183, *183*, 189, 212, *212*, 217

  competition from Knights Templar 61, 62
  in England 119, 217
  establishment of 56–8
  execution of 102
  Fifth Crusade 124
  funding of 88
  at Horns of Hattin, Battle of 100
  and Jerusalem 104, 127
  on Malta 195, 199–205, 208
  militarization of 58–9
  as naval force 138, 140, 157–8, 209
  protection of pilgrims 61–2
  relief of Smyrna 163–4
  and Rhodes 138, 140, 157, *157*, 167–72, 183–9, 191–5
  and Templars' property 153, 154, 156–7
  Third Crusade 106, 107–8
  warships 207–8
Knights of Malta 199
Knights of Saint Peter 45, 47
Knights of St Benedict of Aviz 79
Knights of St Lazarus 75
Knights of St Thomas 109, 157
Knights Templar
  at Acre 130, *130*
  arrests of 146–8, *147*
  at Ascalon (Ashkelon) 93–4
  and banking 119–20, 121
  burning of *134*, *149*, 152, *153*, 154
  castles/properties 86, 88, 95, *95*, 109, *109*, 115, 115–18, *117*, 125, *125*, 128, *136*, 210
  charges against 144–8, 150–3
  clothing 83
  competition from Knights Hospitaller 61, 62
  confessions 153, 154
  on Cyprus 135–7
  daily regime 76
  difficulties facing 137
  disposal of property of 153, 154, 156–7
  education of 33, 35
  in England 95, 115–16, 118, *210*, 217, *217*
  establishment of 61–2, *62*
  execution of 102
  Fifth Crusade 124–6
  funding of 64–7, 83, 88, 90, 95, 114–15, 119–20, *121*
  and Henry II of Jerusalem 136–7

  at Horns of Hattin, Battle of 100–2
  imprisonment of 154
  initiation ceremony *71*, 73–5, *73*
  and Jerusalem *18*, 102, 127
  lack of purpose 141
  military back-up 76
  monastic estates 114–16
  Montgisard 11–13, *12*
  mystic re-imaginings of 214–15
  and Papacy 67
  and Philip IV of France (Philip the Fair) 144–8
  prohibitions 70, 72
  purpose of 62
  recruiting 66
  rules of 70
  scepticism of claims against 148, 150
  Seventh Crusade 127, 129
  support for 66–8
  Third Crusade 106, 107–8
  tribunals 152
Koran 53
Kos *187*

La Valette, Jean Parisot de *200*, 203–5
Lambert de Wattrelos 96
landlords 116
Langan, John 22
Languedoc, France 122–3
Lascaris, Giovanni Paolo 211
Leo IX, Pope 42–4, *42*, 45, *45*, 46, 47
Leo XIII, Pope 212–13
León 78
Leonor Teles 177, 179
Leopold V, Duke of Austria 105, 107
Lepanto, Battle of (1670) 209, *209*
Lisssewege, Belgium 118
Lithuania 132, 173–6
Lombards 143
London *65*, 95, *109*, 116, 118, *210*, 217, *217*
Louis VII, King of France 82–3, *83*
Louis IX, King of France 127, *127*, 128, *128*
Lusignan, Guy de 99, 100, 102, 104
Luther, Martin 195–6, 198
Lydda 15

Maccabeus, Judas 14, *14*
Magnus, Earl 22

al-Mahdi Billah, Abdullah 91
Maille, Jacques de *80*
Malta *212*
    Battle of (1283) 202
    Knights Hospitaller on 195,
        199–205, 208
    Great Siege of (1565) *203–5,*
        203–5
    in later years 212
    Maltese Cross 77, 208, *208*
    Sovereign Military Order of Malta
        77, 216
Mamluks 127–130, 165, 183–4,
    187
al-Mansurah, Battle of (1285) *110,*
    128, 129
Manuel I Komnenos 83, 96
María do Olival Church, Portugal
    182
Martel, Charles *60*
Martelli, Antonio *208*
masculinity 37
masons 213, *213*
Matilda of Boulogne 115
Matthew (Bible) 16–17, 41, 43
medicine 41–2
Mehmed Bey 158
Mehmed II, Sultan 184–5, *185, 186,*
    188
Melisende 87
Mesih Pasha 168–70, *168*
Mesud 158
Milites Sancti Petri 45, 47
Milites Templi 67
Militia Dei 67
mills 118–19
Milvian Bridge, Battle of (312) 19
mining 119
Molay, Jacques de *73,* 135, *146,*
    146, 150, 153–4, *153, 155*
monastic estates 36–42
    Benedictine monks 36–41, 69
    care of the sick 40–2
    Cistercian monks 69
    daily routine in 39
    founding of 36–8
    Knights Templar 114–16
    St Bernard of Clairvaux 69
    St John's hospital, Jerusalem 56–8
    wealth of 39–40
    work 39, *40*
Montagut, Peire de 126
Monte Cassino 38
Montgisard 10–11, *12,* 13, 15,
    99–100

Moors 60, 77–9, 178, 180–1
Morocco 179–81
Al-Mu'azzam Isa 125

Napier, Gordon 147
nation states 65
naval warfare 92, 106, 140, 158,
    160–3, *160–1,* 209, *209*
Nazis 216
Netherlands 199
Nevsky, Prince Alexander 133
Nice, France 207
Nicholas IV, Pope 141, *141*
Nicholson, Helen 154
Nikolaus von Jeroschin 132
Ninth Crusade (1271) 128
Nogaret, Guillaume de 146
Norman conquests 44–5, *45*
Novgorod, Russia 133
Nur ud-Din 97–8, *97*

Omne Datum Optimum 67
Order of Aviz 79, 177, 179–81
Order of Calatrava 78, 178
Order of Christ 150, 181–2
Order of St John 217
Order of St Lazarus 75
Order of St Maurice 184
Orkney 22
Orthodox Christians, Russia 133
Orthodox Church of the East 46
Osorio, Don García de 205
Oultrejordain, Lordships of 56
Outremer 86, 136–7

pageboys 33, 35, *35*
Pallene, Battle of (1344) 162
Parzival/Parsifal 31, 112, 215, 216
Payens, Hugues de *62, 62,* 64–6,
    64–5
Peasants War, Germany (1524–25)
    197–8, *197*
Pedro I of Portugal 177
Pelayo 78, *79*
Penhill, Yorkshire 115
People's Crusade (1096) *49,* 50–1
Perceval (Chrétien) 113–14
Peter I of Cyprus 165
Peter the Hermit *49,* 50
Philip II, King of France 104, 106–7
Philip IV, King of France (Philip the
    Fair) 141–3, *143,* 144–9, *149,*
    151–2, 154, 155
Philip VI, King of France 162
pilgrims, protection of 57–8, 61–2

Pilgrim's Castle, Israel 125, *125*
place names 117
Plötzke, Heinrich von 176
Poincy, Phillippe de Longvilliers de
    211–12
Poitiers, France *60,* 77
Poland 131
Poland and Lithuania 173–6
Portugal 78–9
    empire building 179–83
    knights' property in 118
    Order of Aviz 79, 177, 179–83
preceptories 116, 118–19
privateers 206
property *see* castles/properties
Protestantism 196, 198–9
Prussia 131–2, 173–6

quests 30–1

Ralph de Diceto 9, 11, 13
Rashid ad-Din Sinan *90*
Raymond II of Tripoli, Count *59,*
    89–90
Raymond of Aguilers 53
Raymond of Poitiers, Prince 97
Raymond VI of Toulouse, Count
    123
recruitment of knights 66
Rhodes *138, 140, 157, 183*
    Cem, Sultan 185–9, 188, *188*
    Christians leave 194–5
    early-warning system 187
    as headquarters of Knights
        Hospitaller *138, 140*
    improving defences of 157, *166,*
        183, 189, 192
    and Mamluks 183–4
    siege of (1480) 167–72, 183–4,
        169, 171, 190
    siege of (1522) 192–4, *194*
Richard I, King of England 65
    and Saladin 107
    Third Crusade 104, 106–8, *108*
Rimini, Francesca da 37
Robert de Molesme 69
Robert I, the Count of Artois 129
Rosslyn Chapel, Midlothian *117,*
    189
Ruad, Syria 131, 136
rules of Templars 70
Russia 133

Sablé, Robert de 106
Safed, Syria 128

Saint-Amand, Eudes de 11–13, 99
Saint- Gilles, Raymond de 58, 59
Saladin 11, 98
    early life of 98
    formidable figure 98, 99
    Horns of Hattin, Battle of 100–2
    and Jerusalem 100, 103, 104
    Montgisard 7–14, 99–100
    and Richard I of England 107
    Third Crusade 105, 107–8
Salian Dynasty 42
Samogitians 132
San Servando, Spain 118, 118
Sant'Anna 207–8
Saphadin 124–6
Scotland 116, 117, 152, 189
Second Crusade 80
    failure of 85–6, 88
    France 82–5
    Germany 82, 84
    Knights Templar to take leading
      role 83
    motivation for 81–3
    planning of 83
    recruitment of people 82–3
    Saracens' problems 91
secrecy 75
Sergeac, France 118
Seventh Crusade (1248–54) 127,
    129
sexuality 37
Shia Muslims 91
shipping, attacks on 92, 106, 140,
    158, 160–3, 160–1, 209, 209
Shirkuh, Asad ud-Din 98
Sibylla of Jerusalem, Queen 102
Sicilian Vespers, War of 202
Sicily 44–5, 119, 141, 195, 202
sickness 41–2
Sidon, Lordships of 56
Sigismund I, King of Poland 199
Simonists 74
Sir Galahad 34
Sir Gawain 31
Sir Lancelot 29, 31, 32, 34
Sir Perceval 30–1, 31
Sixth Crusade (1228) 126
Smyrna 163–4
Smyrniote Crusades (1344–51) 162
Sovereign Military Order of Malta
    77, 216
Spain 77–8
    Order of Calatrava 78, 178
    property in 118, 119, 119
squires 35

St Andrew's Church, Temple Grafton
    156
St Anthony Gate, Rhodes 183, 183
St Augustine 20–3, 20
St Benedict of Nursia 38, 38
St Bernard of Clairvaux 41, 66–9,
    68, 69, 81–2, 82
St Francis of Assisi 18, 20
St George 15, 15
St George's Gate, Rhodes 189
St John Ambulance Brigade 217
St John's Gate, London 217, 217
St John's hospital, Jerusalem 56–8,
    56, 104
St Kitts 211–12
St Lazarus 75
St Maurice 184
St Omer, Godfrey de 62, 62, 65
St Peter 43
St Thomas of Canterbury 95
Staunton, Michael 14
Stephen, King 115
Suleiman I, Sultan 191, 192–4, 193,
    195, 203–5
Swingfield, Kent 118
Syria 52, 97, 128, 131
    castle-building 86, 88–9

Tangiers, Siege of 180
Templar Rule 70, 72
Temple Bruer, Lincolnshire 117
Temple Church, London 95, 95, 210
Temple, Cornwall 117
Temple Dinsley, Hertfordshire 117
Temple Ewell, Kent 117
Temple Guiting, Gloucestershire 117
Temple Mount 63
Temple Sowerby, Cumbria 117
Templecombe, Somerset 117
Templetown, County Wexford 117
Teutonic Knights 132
    in Acre 130
    Bailiwick of Utrecht 199
    defection of Master 198–9
    end of 199
    foundation of 105, 105
    modern world 215–16
    Peasants War 197–8
    in Prussia 131–3, 173–6, 174–5
textile industry 118
Theobald II of Champagne, Count
    83
Third Crusade (1189–92)
    Acre 105–7
    aftermath of 108–9

    as Crusade of Kings 104–5
    and Germany 105
    inconclusive result 108
Toledo, Spain 119
Tomar, Portugal 118, 181–3
torture 146, 147
training of knights 33, 35
Tremelay, Bernard de 90, 94
trial of Templars 147–8
Tripoli, as Crusader State 54, 55, 56
Troyes, Chrétien de 31, 113
True Cross 10, 10, 13, 101, 102
Turnashah, Al-Muazzam 127
Tyre 102, 104, 107

Umar, Caliph 48
Umur Bey 162
Urban II, Pope 47–8, 47, 50
Urban IV, Pope 202
Urban V, Pope 165, 165

Vasco de Gama 182, 182
Venice 120, 122, 161–2
Vézelay, France 82
Villaret, Fulk de 138, 139
Villiers, Jean de 130–1, 131
Villiers de l'Isle-Adam, Philippe 192,
    192, 195, 195
Visigoths 78
Vitry-le-François 83
Vox in Excelso 153

Wagner, Richard 215
Walter of Brienne 127
war, religious justification for 20–3
War Council of Acre (1148) 85
warships 124, 124, 158–9, 159,
    207–8
weapons 172
Wife of Bath 37
Wilhelm II of Germany, Kaiser 216
William II 44
William of Tyre 14, 14, 53, 62,
    85–6, 92, 94, 98
William of Wykeham 35
Wladyslaw I, King 176
Women
    and chivalry 28–9, 29
    and knights 31–3, 34
    and sexual desires 37
    temptations of 72

Zara 120
Zengi, Imad ad-Din 81, 91, 97

PICTURE CREDITS